AUSABLE ALLIGATORS

Here's what readers from around the country are saying about Johnathan Rand's *AMERICAN CHILLERS:*

"Our whole class just finished reading 'Poisonous Pythons Paralyze Pennsylvania, and it was GREAT!"
                                                        -Trent J., age 11, Pennsylvania

"I finished reading "Dangerous Dolls of Delaware in just three days! It creeped me out!
                                                        -Brittany K., age 9, Ohio

"My teacher read GHOST IN THE GRAVEYARD to us. I loved it! I can't wait to read GHOST IN THE GRAND!"
                                                        -Nicholas H., age 8, Arizona

"My brother got in trouble for reading your book after he was supposed to go to bed. He says it's your fault, because your books are so good. But he's not mad at you or anything."
                                                        -Ariel C., age 10, South Carolina

"Thank you for coming to our school. I thought you would be scary, but you were really funny."
                                                        -Tyler D., age 10, Michigan

"American Chillers is my favorite series! Can you write them faster so I don't have to wait for the next one? Thank you."
                                                        -Alex W., age 8, Washington, D.C.

"I can't stop reading AMERICAN CHILLERS! I've read every one twice, and I'm going to read them again!"
                                                        -Emilee T., age 12, Wisconsin

"Our whole class listened to CREEPY CAMPFIRE
CHILLERS with the lights out. It was really spooky!"

-*Erin J., age 12, Georgia*

"When you write a book about Oklahoma, write it about my
city. I've lived here all my life, and it's a freaky place."

-*Justin P., age 11, Oklahoma*

"When you came to our school, you said that all of your books
are true stories. I don't believe you, but I LOVE your books,
anyway!"

-*Anthony H., age 11, Ohio*

"I really liked NEW YORK NINJAS! I'm going to get all of
your books!"

-*Chandler L., age 10, New York*

"Every night I read your books in bed with a flashlight. You
write really creepy stories!"

-*Skylar P., age 8, Michigan*

"My teacher let me borrow INVISIBLE IGUANAS OF
ILLINOIS, and I just finished it! It was really, really great!"

-*Greg R., age 11, Virginia*

"I went to your website and saw your dogs. They are really
cute. Why don't you write a book about them?"

-*Laura L., age 10, Arkansas*

"DANGEROUS DOLLS OF DELAWARE was so scary that I
couldn't read it at night. Then I had a bad dream. That book
was super-freaky!"

-*Sean F., age 9, Delaware*

"I have every single book in the CHILLERS series, and I love them!"

-Mike W., age 11, Michigan

"Your books rock!"

-Darrell D., age 10, Minnesota

"My friend let me borrow one of your books, and now I can't stop! So far, my favorite is WISCONSIN WEREWOLVES. That was a great book!"

-Riley S., age 12, Oregon

"I read your books every single day. They're COOL!"

-Katie M., age 12, Michigan

"I just found out that the #14 book is called CREEPY CONDORS OF CALIFORNIA. That's where I live! I can't wait for this book!"

-Emilio H., age 10, California

"I have every single book that you've written, and I can't decide which one I love the most! Keep writing!"

-Jenna S., age 9, Kentucky

"I love to read your books! My brother does, too!"

-Joey B., age 12, Missouri

"I got IRON INSECTS INVADE INDIANA for my birthday, and it's AWESOME!"

-Colin T., age 10, Indiana

#12:
AuSable
Alligators

Johnathan
Rand

An AudioCraft Publishing, Inc. book

Michigan Chillers #12: AuSable Alligators
ISBN 1-893699-85-4

Cover Illustrations by Dwayne Harris
Cover layout and design by Sue Harring

Printed in USA

First Printing - November 2005

AUSABLE
ALLIGATORS

VISIT THE OFFICIAL WORLD HEADQUARTERS OF AMERICAN CHILLERS & MICHIGAN CHILLERS!

The all-new HOME for books by Johnathan Rand! Featuring books, hats, shirts, bookmarks and other cool stuff not available anywhere else in the world! Plus, watch the American Chillers website for news of special events and signings at *CHILLERMANIA* with author Johnathan Rand! Located in northern lower Michigan, on I-75 just off exit 313!

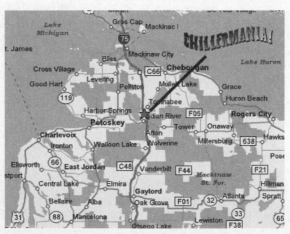

www.americanchillers.com

1

The final rays of sun bled through thick pine trees. Stars began to twinkle in the darkening sky.

Perfect, I thought.

Around me, water babbled. I was in the middle of the AuSable River with my fly rod in hand.

Alone.

Even better. No crowds, no one to disturb my fishing.

My name is Craig Pierce, and I live in Grayling. Actually, we live out of town a bit. There are not many houses where we live . . . just forest. Lots of pine, oak, maple, quaking aspen, and cedar trees. In fact, the nearest house is almost a quarter of a mile away. It belongs to the Penrose family. They live in Pontiac, which is about a four hour drive south. Heather Penrose is twelve, which is how old I am. In the summer, we fly fish together. She's pretty cool, and I wish she didn't live so far away, because I knew she would love to be trout fishing tonight.

You see, the night was *perfect*. It was warm, and I was catching quite a few fish. Nothing big, yet . . . but that was about to change.

If there's one single thing I love more than anything, it's fly fishing for trout. The AuSable River is a famous trout stream, with lots of brook trout and brown trout. My dad taught me how to fly fish when I was nine, and I've been hooked ever since.

(Except in the winter, of course. Grayling gets a lot of snow in the winter, and it gets really cold!)

But during the summer, on nights like tonight, I was right at home. I was wearing my rubber waders, which come up to my chest and allow me to walk in the water without getting wet. I also had on my vest, which carries my fly boxes, leaders, a spare line, a small penlight, a net, and some insect repellant. That's another thing you need if you fly fish the AuSable: bug spray. Otherwise, the mosquitos and black flies will eat you alive.

But tonight, I would encounter something else that could quite possibly eat me alive.

Not a mosquito.

Not a black fly.

Not a snake or a lizard or anything else I could have possibly imagined.

In fact, if I would have known then what I know now, I probably wouldn't have set foot in the river.

A bat flitted past, spinning and squealing as it hunted for bugs. Water rippled, and I took a step downstream. Gravel crunched beneath my rubber-soled waders, and the sound was muted by the gurgling river. A choir of crickets and frogs sang from the shadowy river bank.

I cast my fly, laying out the line so that it skirted beneath the overhanging branches of a cedar tree.

Fly fishing is a lot different than most types of fishing, in that you don't cast like a normal fishing pole. Instead, you strip out line and use the rod to bring all of the line into the air at the same time, back and behind you. Then you cast the line forward, and drop the fly into the water. Once you get the hang of it, it's a lot of fun.

Dark shadows lurked like silent monsters along the banks of the river. Normally, it would be hard for most people to fly fish the AuSable after dark, but I knew the river like the back of my hand . . . even when it was late at night. I knew where the deep holes were, and where the sunken logs and rocks were. I knew where the trees hung out over the water, so I wouldn't get my fly caught on a limb. I knew where the big fish lurked, too.

And I love fishing the AuSable after dark, after most other fishermen have gone home. Nighttime on the AuSable River is when big brown trout come out of the deep holes. They swim to shallower water, near the banks, in search of food. It's the best time to fish, but it's also the most challenging.

And, I make my own flies. The technique is called fly tying, and I make flies using a bare hook, thread, and animal fur and bird feathers. Oh, there are a lot of other things you can use, but mostly, flies are tied with natural fur and feathers.

Although it was too dark to see where my fly had landed, I heard the thin *plop!* as it hit the water. I knew it had landed right where I wanted it.

I let the current pull the line, and I gave the rod a few twitches. I was using a new fly pattern, one that I had made up on my own. I had never used this particular fly before, so I wasn't sure how well it would work. Some flies work better than others at different times.

Suddenly, the water exploded about thirty feet away, right where my fly was! It was so sudden and unexpected that I almost jumped out of my waders! There was a sharp pull on my fly rod, and I held it tight, giving it a tug to set the hook.

The rod bent, and I knew I had a fish on.

Boy . . . was I in for a surprise!

I was sure I had hooked into a big brown trout. He was a real fighter, too, sweeping back and forth across the river, diving into a deep hole, and then heading downstream. Once, he leapt all the way out of the water. I caught only a glimpse of him in the darkness . . . but it was enough to tell me that something wasn't right. I couldn't put my finger on it, but I was sure of it: something wasn't quite right with this brown trout.

I battled for nearly ten minutes before the fish grew tired. In the darkness, I still couldn't see the fish. I pulled him closer and closer, holding my fly rod high with my right hand. My penlight was clipped to my vest, and I turned it on with my left hand. Then I readied the net.

Just a little bit closer . . . .

The fish splashed at the surface, then dove down again. I tried to scoop him up into my net, but I missed.

Carefully, I brought him close again. The fish was really fighting! I extended the net out a bit farther, waiting for him to get nearer so I wouldn't miss. After all, I didn't want to get him so close . . . only to have him break the line.

In the beam of my small penlight, I saw the fish. I seized the opportunity and plunged the net into the water.

Got him!

Although I couldn't see him, I could tell by the weight in the net that he wasn't going to get away. The fish was securely in the net.

I pulled the net from the water, held it beneath the glowing light . . . and gasped at what I was holding.

The thing in my net wasn't a brown trout.

It wasn't a brook trout.

It was the biggest rainbow trout I had ever seen in the AuSable! Now, I know that might not seem like a big deal to *you,* but, where I live, there aren't many rainbow trout. I only catch a couple of them a year, and I've never caught any big ones.

But this fish was beautiful! He was almost twenty inches long. He was covered with colorful spots. A bright pink and orange band ran along his side.

"Wow," I said out loud, marveling at my catch.

The fish made a sudden thrash in the net, splashing water all over.

"Hold on, buddy," I said, and I tucked my fly rod under my right arm to give me a free hand. Then I dunked my hand into the water to get it wet. Before you handle a fish, it's a good idea to get your hand wet, so that your dry skin doesn't injure him.

I reached into the net and picked up the trout. He struggled and squirmed, but I was able to pull him out of the net without a problem.

I held the fish beneath my light, and again marveled at his size and color.

And on my new fly, too! One that I had created!

Cool beans.

Carefully, I unhooked the fly from the trout's mouth. It took a moment, because the fish kept struggling to get away. Once, my rod almost fell from under my arm.

After the trout was unhooked, I took one more long look at him. He sure was a beautiful fish, and I was really proud of myself.

Gently, I lowered him into the rustling river. As soon as his belly touched the surface, he gave a powerful thrash with his tail and vanished into the dark water, to live another day and perhaps be caught by another fisherman.

It was then that I noticed something.

The night had become deathly silent. The crickets had stopped chirping, and the frogs were no longer croaking. The only thing I could hear was the rippling river as it rushed around my waders in the waist-deep waters.

Strange.

I looked up into the night sky. The dark silhouettes of trees rose up like tribal lances, obscuring many of the stars. The trail of the milky way curled across the heavens.

But there were no sounds.

Except . . . .

An odd sound from downstream caught my attention. It was a repetitive, whooshing sound, and it was very faint.

But it quickly became louder.

Louder.

Louder, still . . . .

And it sounded like—

Like *wings*.

My tiny penlight was useless, because the beam only shone a few feet in front of me.

The sound grew louder still.

But when I saw what was making the sound, I knew that it was already too late to get away.

The thing coming at me was huge! I caught a glimpse of giant wings, just above the water. It was terrible.

There was nothing else I could do but duck down into the water. I knew I would get soaked and water would fill my waders, but it would be a lot better than being carried away by that awful flying beast!

I bent over and fell into the water . . . just as the giant wings flapped over my head. The creature let out a terrible screech, and I knew that I probably scared it more than it had scared me.

In the next instant, the creature had passed. I was still in the water, and I turned to look upstream. I could see its dark shadow, and it was then that I realized what it was: a great blue heron, a very large bird that is pretty common on the AuSable, and a lot of other rivers and lakes in Michigan and surrounding states. In fact, if you live near water in Michigan, there's a good chance you've seen a blue heron . . . so you know just how big they are.

I shook my head and laughed, struggling to stand up. Cold water had gushed into my waders, making them heavy and awkward.

"Great, Craig," I whispered. *"It'll be a cold walk home."*

Water dripped from my hat, my vest, my fly rod, and my arms. I was completely soaked. When I got home, I would have to take everything out of my vest so it could dry.

But it could have been worse. If the blue heron had hit me, we both could have been in big trouble. I could have been seriously hurt, along with the bird.

However, now I had something else to worry about.

The bird had come upon me so suddenly that I had dropped my fly into the water. The current had carried it downstream, where it was dangling in the middle of the river at the end of my leader.

A leader is a thin strand of monofilament that is tied to the fly line. It's usually between six and twelve feet long. Because the actual line is thick, a thin, nearly invisible leader is used so that the fish won't see it attached to the fly. Trout have good eyes, and you have to work hard to fool them.

But that's not what the problem was.

The problem came when I began to reel in the line.

That's when the water exploded, and my fly rod was nearly yanked out of my hand. I gave it a tug—more out of surprise than anything—and felt the hook take hold.

My rod bent so far that I thought it was going to break.

Up until that point, I had planned on going home. I was cold and wet, and it was getting late.

Now, however, I was going to battle yet another fish.

At least, that's what I *thought*. I had no reason to suspect that what had struck my fly wasn't a fish. I was sure it was a big brown trout or, maybe, another rainbow.

I had no idea that what was on the other end of the line wasn't even a fish . . . nor did I realize the danger that was only moments away.

I quickly forgot about how cold and wet I was. I forgot about the great blue heron that had scared me.

The only thing I could think about was landing the fish at the end of my line.

But there was something strange about the way the fish was fighting. It didn't feel like it was big—probably not as big as the rainbow trout I had caught—but the fish was very sluggish. Usually, a trout will dart and dive all over the place, trying to break the line and get away.

This fish, however, didn't do that. It was slow in its movements, and it had yet to come to the surface. The fish seemed to want to dive into a deep hole and lay there like a log.

I struggled to bring him closer. I succeeded a few times . . . but every time I drew him near, he took off again. I had to let line out so that the fish wouldn't break it.

Wow, I thought. *Two big fish in one night! Wait until I tell Mom and Dad!*

Gradually, I was able to bring the fish closer. He had yet to surface, so I had no idea what kind he was . . . but I was sure he was a big ol' brown. He fought sluggishly, but I had no reason to think that what I was fighting would be anything but a fish.

Until I caught a glimpse of him in my penlight.

It was only a flash, for a quick moment.

But what I saw didn't look like the colors of a brown trout.

Or a rainbow trout.

It was too big to be a brook trout.

And was I mistaken . . . or did the fish look like it had . . . *scales?* Trout have scales, but they are so small that it can be hard to see them. The scales that this fish had were big and noticeable.

It took another dive into deeper water, and I let out more line. But already, I could sense the fish getting tired. It wouldn't be long before I had him in my net.

Soon, the fish was almost within reach. I held the net in one hand and my fly rod in the other, slowly working the fish closer. He was still hidden in the dark, churning water, and I knew that, as soon as he surfaced, I would have to be quick with the net.

Gently, I raised my fly rod higher, bringing the fish closer to the surface. My other hand was ready with the net.

Suddenly, the creature appeared.

Immediately, I was gripped by shock and fear. Panic instantly set in as I gazed at what was on the line.

Dark, beady eyes glared at me. Razor-sharp teeth shined in the beam of my penlight. Dark, ruddy brown scales glistened.

I knew that what I was seeing couldn't be real.

It couldn't be true.

But it was.

Right here, in the AuSable River, at the end of my line with a fly hooked in its mouth, was an alligator! He wasn't very big—maybe about the size of the rainbow trout I'd caught earlier—but that didn't mean the creature wasn't dangerous.

I wanted to throw down my net, toss my rod into the water and run. I had to get away, out of the water. I had to get home. Mom and Dad would know what to do.

But before I could even react, the alligator opened its jaws even wider. It hissed loudly . . . and with a powerful swish of its tail, the beast lunged right at me!

Fear—tight, crippling, all-out terror—grabbed me and held me frozen. The alligator attacked so fast that I didn't have time to move.

In fact, I probably couldn't have moved if I tried. My waders were still filled with water, and it was like trying to move in cement.

Fortunately, I realized after a moment that the creature wasn't attacking me, and he wasn't trying to bite me. He was just struggling to get away.

For a moment, I thought he was going to be caught in the net, but with a powerful snap of his jaws his teeth cut the netting, and the creature was free. It dove into the dark water, but it still had my fly hooked in its mouth . . . which meant that I still had him on the line!

I wanted no part of this anymore.

One of the tools I carry in my vest is a pair of fingernail clippers. I quickly found them and cut the line.

The alligator was free. That didn't necessarily mean that I was out of danger, and the sooner I could get out of the river, the better.

I trudged to the riverbank. With my waders so heavy with water, I was quickly puffing and panting. After all . . . I was carrying an additional fifty pounds in my waders.

When I reached the shore, I stripped off my wet vest and hung it on a branch. Then I unhooked the suspenders that held my waders up. As my waders crumpled around my waist, water poured out.

My penlight, still clipped to my vest that was hanging on the branch, cast a small beam on the ground. I wondered if the alligator was gone.

I stepped out of my waders, picked them up, then turned them upside down to empty the remaining water. Then I slipped back into them, hooked my suspenders, and put on my vest.

Then, and only then, did I start to calm down a little.

But I still had a billion questions.

How did an alligator get into the AuSable River? Were there any more? If so, how big were they? It had a rounded snout, so I knew it was an alligator and not a crocodile. Crocodiles have faces that are pointed, while alligators' faces are more round. I saw that on television.

Using my light, I quickly found the trail that snaked along the side of the river. It would only take me about fifteen minutes to walk through the forest, even in all of my fishing gear.

But I couldn't wait. I walked as fast as I could, and my wet clothing squished with every movement. As I made my way along the dark trail, I began to think about how I would explain the alligator to my mom and dad.

And the more that I thought about it, the more I realized something.

There was no way in the world Mom and Dad were going to believe me. Not a chance. When I got home and told them I'd caught an alligator, Mom and Dad would laugh. In my mind, I could hear my dad.

There are no alligators in the AuSable, Craig, he would say. *You probably just caught some other kind of fish.*

As I thought about it, I began to wonder.

Was it really an alligator? How could it be? Alligators live in the south . . . not the north. They like warm water, and the AuSable is very cold.

Is it possible? I wondered. *Did I just imagine it? Maybe it was some strange kind of fish, or perhaps a lizard. After all, it was very dark, and all I had was my tiny penlight. Maybe, in the murky dark, I had only* thought *that I had seen an alligator. Maybe—*

A noise in the bushes, just off the trail, caused me to stop. My heart beat faster. I swept the beam in the place where I thought the noise had come from.

Alligators don't always live in the water, I thought. *They live on the land, too, and—*

In the forest.

The noise came again.

Now, I don't scare very easily. I fish at night a lot, so I'm used to being surprised by a raccoon or a porcupine. Once, I came upon a deer that had been sleeping. When the animal got up and ran off, it made all kinds of noise, and I really freaked out.

But it hadn't *scared* me. I wasn't scared, because I knew that there was nothing in the woods that would come after me.

However, after what I'd seen in the river, I wasn't so sure.

Bushes rustled. I heard them, and I saw movement in the murky glow of my penlight. Unfortunately, my tiny little penlight wasn't very bright, and the branches and brush were veiled in dark shadows.

I decided to keep going. It was probably a small animal of some sort . . . certainly nothing that could hurt me.

I began trudging through the brush . . . and that's when I felt the vicelike grip around my right ankle.

I screamed, and my shrill cry pierced the night. Whatever held my leg wasn't letting go, and I struggled to break free. I could imagine the sharp teeth of the alligator, puncturing my rubber waders and digging into my leg.

I spun and broke free, and was just about to run—

That's when I heard giggling.

Laughter.

A girl.

Twigs snapped. Branches moved. My heart was racing, and my breathing was heavy.

"Gotcha!" I heard. Instantly, I knew who it was: Heather Penrose, my friend from Pontiac.

She let go of my leg and climbed out from the bushes where she'd been hiding. Even in the dull of night, I could see the huge grin on her face. Her dark brown hair had a few leaves and a couple small branches stuck in it.

I was furious! She had really scared me!

Aiming my penlight at her, I stood on the trail, trying to catch my breath. "What did you do *that* for?!?!" I demanded. I was really mad.

"That was great!" she boasted, placing her hands on her hips. "You were really scared! I finally got you back!"

"What are you talking about?!?!" I fumed. "Got me back for what?"

"Remember last year?" she asked. "Remember when we were roasting marshmallows with my family? My dad was telling us a spooky story, and you jumped out of the woods and scared me?"

I remembered. I had hid in the woods, and waited until the time was right. Then I jumped out and scared Heather . . . and everyone else, too.

"Yeah, but—" I started to say, but Heather interrupted.

"Yeah, but *nothing*," she said, pointing a finger at me. "I told you I was going to get you back." She placed her hands on her hips. "And now, I did!"

Heather was right. If I had scared her, I guess I should have expected that it would only be fair if she scared me, too.

"Okay," I said, managing a smile. "You got me back. Now we're even. Fair?"

"Fair," she said, pulling the leaves and sticks out of her hair. "Geez . . . I didn't think you'd be fishing for this long. I've been hiding in these bushes for an hour, waiting for you to walk by the trail! I thought the mosquitos were going to carry me away."

Heather told me that her family had arrived from Pontiac earlier in the evening, and that they would be spending a whole week at their cabin.

"A whole week?!?!" I exclaimed.

She bobbed her head. "We can fly fish every day!"

We were going to have a blast, that was for sure. We always did when we went fishing together. I knew the coming week would be a lot of fun.

What I didn't know was that what I had seen in the river wasn't my imagination.

I didn't know that I'd actually hooked a real, live alligator.

And I didn't know that there were more.

It was only a matter of time before my world was turned upside down.

I didn't tell Heather about the alligator that night. I knew that there was no way she would believe me.

And I didn't tell my mom or dad. I was *sure* there was no way they would believe me.

But, then again . . . I wasn't sure if *I* even believed *myself*. The whole notion of an alligator in the AuSable River, a famous trout stream, seemed ridiculous. Everyone would laugh at me. Nobody would believe a twelve-year-old kid.

Unless I had proof.

First, I had to convince myself. I had to know for sure. Had I really hooked an alligator? Could it possibly have been something else? Sometimes, your mind can play tricks on you. Maybe that's what happened to me.

The very next morning, I hiked back to where I'd hooked the 'alligator' . . . or whatever it was. I didn't know what I would find, but I was going to look for evidence . . . maybe even the alligator itself. If I had proof, then people would believe me. I took a small, disposable camera with me . . . just in case. If I *did* see the alligator, I wanted to have a picture. Then, people would *have* to believe me.

I hiked through the forest, leaving my fishing gear in the shed. I decided to stay out of the water until I proved to myself once and for all that what I'd seen had only been my imagination. After all . . . if what I saw was a *real* alligator, I wasn't going near the river again!

In a few minutes, I was at the spot on the river where I'd seen the creature. The morning was overcast and warm, the sky was dark and gray, and it looked like it might rain at any moment. Mosquitos buzzed by my head. I forgot to put bug spray on, so the tiny insects were doing everything they could to get at my skin. They were like little buzzing vampires. I waved them away with a careless swish of my arm. Mosquitos didn't bother me so much, when there might be something else to worry about!

I stopped at the riverbank and stared. Water lapped at the shore, curling around logs and rocks. A duck drifted by. When he saw me, he took flight with a splashing burst and angry quacks. A mosquito landed on my ear, and I waved him away.

My eyes scanned the bank on the other side of the river, searching beneath the low limbs for the alligator. I was certain that if the creature was on a log or in the weeds near the shore, I would be able to spot him. I held my camera up, ready to click off a picture.

But—

Nothing. I didn't see anything that looked even *close* to what an alligator looked like.

Rain started to fall, but I hardly noticed it. I kept searching the riverbank, gazing into the river, looking for any sign of the slithering reptile that I'd hooked the night before. I peered into the brush around my feet, just to make sure that the creature wasn't there. He wasn't . . . but something else was.

Tracks.

In the black, gooey mud.

Tracks like I had never seen before.

And, in between the tracks, a long, curving line . . . which could only be the hallmark of a dragging tail.

An alligator's tail.

I knelt down to get a closer look, and there was no mistaking it. While I wasn't exactly sure what alligator tracks look like, I was sure the tracks in the mud weren't from any other animals in the area. We don't have big lizards in Michigan, and there's nothing else I know of that could make tracks like that.

The rain began to fall harder, soaking my shirt. A droplet of water ran off my hair and down my cheek. I was still kneeling, but now I turned my head up and looked around, placing my hand to my forehead to shield my eyes from the heavy rain.

Now, I knew. Now, I was sure.

I really *did* have an alligator on my line last night. There was nothing else it could have been, and right at my feet was the proof I needed.

But my proof was vanishing before my eyes.

I stood up suddenly. *"Oh, no!"* I cried. *"Oh, no!"*

The rain had become heavier and was washing away the tracks! The mud at my feet was very soft, and the rain was making the tracks vanish!

I quickly took a couple of pictures, but I knew that they wouldn't turn out. In seconds, the tracks were gone. Oh, there were some small indentations in the mud, but they no longer looked like the tracks of an alligator.

Now I was mad. I wished I would have told Heather about the alligator. She might not have believed me last night, but if she would have been with me now, she, too, would have seen the tracks for herself.

I watched the raindrops dance on the river, creating a sheen of foamy white bubbles. I was soaked, but it didn't bother me at all.

Because I had a plan.

That alligator had tried to eat the fly I was fishing with. That meant that I had fooled him.

And if I had fooled him once . . . .

Maybe I could do it again. Maybe, if I was more prepared, I could actually catch him.

Something in the back of my mind told me it wasn't a good idea. It was a little voice that whispered that it was a dangerous idea, that it might get me into a lot of trouble.

I ignored it.

I shouldn't have.

Soon, I would find out that the little voice was right.

When I returned home, I made six more flies that were identical to the fly I was using when I hooked the alligator. They were actually kind of cool looking. That's one thing I liked about tying my own flies: I could create any kind of fly I wanted, in any color. Plus, it costs a lot less to make a fly than it does to buy them in the store.

After I finished, I rode my bike to Heather's house. I was going to tell her about the alligator, and about the tracks I'd found that morning . . . but she wasn't home. Her mom said that she went into town with her older brother and her dad, and they wouldn't be back until later in the evening.

It was already three o'clock. It was still cloudy, but the rain had stopped. Everything was fresh and green, and the air was heavy and damp. I didn't know if alligators came out in the daytime or not, but I had a couple of hours before I'd have to be home for dinner. I figured I might as well go fishing by myself, back to the same spot where I'd first spotted the alligator.

"I'm going fishing, Mom," I said, as I opened the front door. I didn't go inside. I just popped my head in far enough to shout.

"Don't be gone very long," Mom shouted back from the kitchen. "We're having spaghetti for dinner."

Cool beans. I *love* spaghetti.

I parked my bike in the garage and walked to the shed where I store my fishing gear. I had hung my waders upside down in the shed, and, thankfully, they had dried. I put them on, snapped my suspenders, and slipped into my vest. In no time at all I was wading in the middle of the river, casting my fly, slowly making my way downstream.

But I kept my eye out. Even though I had to wade past a couple of bends to get to the spot where I'd hooked the alligator and spotted the tracks, it was possible that he could be anywhere. The thought made me kind of nervous, but I wasn't really scared in the daylight. If I saw the creature before he saw me, there was a good chance that I would be able to get away.

I cast the fly toward the riverbank, letting the current catch the line and pull it to the center of the stream. When the fly reached the middle of the river I repeated the process, casting to the other side of the river. All the while I kept moving, slowly heading downstream. Rippling water rushed against my waders, gently urging me along. Gravel crunched beneath the rubber soles of my boots.

Up ahead, sitting at the very top of a limbless, dead tree, was a kingfisher. It's a bird that is a little

49

bigger than a blue jay, with a longer bill. They feed on small fish, and, while I watched, the bird dipped from its post and plunged straight down, down, into the water. A second later it emerged, flying off with a small fish in its beak. I wish I could catch fish that easily.

Finally, I approached the bend where I'd hooked the alligator. In the daylight, it was a lot easier to see everything. It was hard to imagine that, last night, I'd been scared out of my wits. As I looked around, I wondered how on earth I could have been so frightened. Everything seemed so calm and peaceful in the daytime.

But, then again, it had been dark. It had been dark, and I had an alligator on my line. I had good reason to be freaked out.

I peered under tree limbs, searching the riverbank. I looked at the long, wisping seaweed that waved in the current, and I let the fly drag in the middle of the river.

I didn't see anything that looked out of the ordinary. Not that I had really expected to, but still . . . .

I cast the fly toward the riverbank, trying to loop it beneath a low hanging cedar branch. As good as I could guess, that's where I had cast my fly last night, when the alligator had gone after it. I let out a bit too much line, though, and the fly caught on a leafy branch. I tugged several times, and the fly came free.

My next cast was perfect. The fly followed a tight loop of line and leader, slipping under the branches and landing with a heavy *plop!* in the dark pool of backwater.

The current caught the line, pulling the fly. I let it drag downstream, giving the rod a twitch every few seconds. By doing so, the fly would appear to flutter, making it look alive. I let the fly drift to the middle of the river, but—

Nothing.

I tried again, on the other side of the stream.

Still nothing.

Then, back to the other side. The fly landed in the water, right where I wanted it to.

Suddenly—

Ka-whoosh!

The water exploded, and there was a tight pull on my fly rod. I raised it up to set the hook, and it was almost yanked out of my hands.

My heart hammered.

Oh my gosh! I thought. *Oh my gosh! I really did it! I've hooked him! I've hooked him again!*

Although I couldn't see the creature, I could find him by looking at where my line met the water. The alligator dove into a deep hole in the bend of the river. Actually, the hole was only about six feet deep, but it was still over my head. I was always careful to avoid wading into it . . . especially at night.

Now that I had the creature on the line again, I wasn't all that sure what I was going to do. What if the alligator tried to bite me?

Either way, I had to prove it to myself. I wanted to see the creature again, with my own eyes, during the daylight. If I had hooked into it again and saw that it really *was* an alligator, I could just cut the line. I'd figure out what to do from there. I'd call the police, as I was sure they would want to know about it. After all, an alligator in the AuSable could cause all kinds of problems. There are many people who fly fish and canoe the river, and I don't think they'd appreciate being attacked by a vicious alligator.

My fly rod was still bent over as I battled the beast. It turned another direction and went back into shallower water.

Suddenly, it came into view, and my heart stopped thrashing. It wasn't an alligator, after all. It was a brown trout. A good-sized fish at that, but I was kind of disappointed that it wasn't an alligator.

It took me a few minutes to land the trout. After I let him go, I paused for a moment to look around. I searched the riverbank again, peering around and under bushes, logs, and branches. I gazed into the clear, rippling waters, looking for any sign of the alligator.

Nothing.

But as I looked into the deep hole that flowed around the elbow of the river, I wondered something.

Suppose the alligator is there, right now? What if he's at the bottom of the river, hiding in seaweed, among logs and rocks?

From where I was, I couldn't see into the hole. It was too deep and too dark.

But if I used my mask and snorkel . . . .

I have a mask, snorkel, and fins that I use when I go swimming. In the river, it's a lot of fun. It's like looking into another world. I see different kinds of fish and things you wouldn't normally see when you're swimming.

Yeah, I thought. *If I came back here with my mask, snorkel, and fins . . . .*

But not alone. I would get Heather to come with me. It would be safer with two of us.

I sloshed to the riverbank, stepped out of the stream, and followed the trail through the forest, back to my house. After hanging up my gear in the shed, I went into my house and got cleaned up.

During dinner, we talked about my sister, who was away at summer camp. I told Mom and Dad I had made a new fly pattern that really worked great . . . but I didn't tell them I'd hooked an alligator with it.

"Have you ever seen any strange lizards in the river?" I asked Dad.

"Lizards?" Dad said, as he reached for the pepper.

"Yeah," I said. "Lizards."

Dad shook his head. "No, I've never seen any lizards around. I don't think we have lizards in Grayling. The only thing I've seen are salamanders. Why? Did you see one?"

"No, I don't think so," I said. "I think it was just a fish. But, at first, I thought it was a lizard. Or, maybe a . . . ."

I didn't finish my sentence, and my dad looked up. "A what?" he asked.

"Oh, nothing," I said. "It was only a fish."

Right after we'd finished eating, the phone rang. It was Heather.

"Hey," I said, "I've got to tell you about something that I saw last night."

"What?" she replied.

I was going to tell her about the alligator, but I figured it would be better if I told her face-to-face.

"It's important," I said, "and I want to tell you in person."

"Well, I can't come over tonight," Heather said. "We're going into town to see a movie. How about in the morning?"

"That's cool," I said. "See you tomorrow."

As I hung up the phone, I wondered if she would believe me. When I told her what I'd spotted—or, at least, what I *thought* I'd spotted—she would probably laugh.

No, the only way she would believe me would be to have absolute proof.

Well, we'd have our proof, all right . . . a lot sooner than I thought.

In the morning, I called Heather to see if she wanted to swim.

"No way," she said. "The river is freezing!"

"Oh, it's not *that* bad," I replied. "Besides, there's something I've got to tell you."

"What?" she asked.

"Come on over," I said, "and I'll tell you."

"Okay," she said. "I'll see you in a few minutes."

She met me at the shed. She was carrying a beach towel and a bottle of water. Her hair was tied back in a pony tail, and she was wearing a

Detroit Red Wings baseball cap. I was in the shed, gathering up my snorkeling gear, and I had just told her that I'd caught an alligator the night before last.

"You caught a *what?!?!*" Heather asked.

"An alligator," I repeated. "Actually, I didn't really catch it. But he went after my fly. I had him in my net, but after I found out what it was, I cut the line. I was going to tell you about it last night, but I didn't think you'd believe me."

Heather looked shocked. "Are you sure it wasn't a lizard, or maybe a salamander?"

"Positive," I replied with a nod. "I've never seen an alligator before, except on television or in a book . . . but I know what they look like. And there was no way this thing was anything but an alligator."

"You're really serious, aren't you?" she asked.

"Yes," I replied confidently.

"And you want to go for a *swim?*" Heather asked incredulously. "Are you nuts?"

"Well, like I said . . . the alligator wasn't very big. There is no way the thing could eat us or anything."

And I was right about that. The alligator that I'd hooked two nights before wasn't big enough to eat us.

But there were others that *were* big enough . . . and Heather and I were about to find them.

12

It was quicker to walk down the trail to the place where I'd first spotted the alligator, so that's what we did. I carried my snorkeling gear in a large beach bag. As we traipsed through the forest, we talked and wondered aloud how an alligator wound up in the AuSable River.

"Maybe someone had it as a pet, and it got too big," Heather suggested. "I've heard that some people have done that. I heard about someone who let their alligator loose in a lake, and it grew to almost six feet long."

"Maybe," I said. "Whatever the reason, he shouldn't be here. Somebody is going to get hurt."

Soon, we came to a bend in the river . . . the place where I'd first hooked the alligator two nights ago.

"I was standing right over there," I said, pointing. "I was fishing. It was after dark, and I cast my fly over there. That's where I hooked him. At first, I thought it was a big trout. But when I got him closer, I realized that it wasn't a fish at all."

We gazed into the river, searching for the alligator, but he wasn't there. Or, if he was, he was hiding . . . and maybe he was hiding in the deep pool on the far side of the stream.

"I'm not going in there," Heather whispered, shaking her head. "I don't have a mask or a snorkel, and I wouldn't go if I did. Not if there's an alligator hanging around somewhere."

"Well, it's a long shot," I said. "But think about it: if we *do* find out that there's an alligator in the river, we'll be famous. We might even be on television!"

"Yeah, if the alligator doesn't eat us," Heather said glumly.

I took off my shoes and socks, then stepped into the river. It was chilly! Goose bumps formed on my legs while I slipped into my fins. Then I put my mask on over my head and pulled it over my face.

"Be careful," Heather said, as I slowly walked farther into the stream.

The water got deeper, and I stopped in the middle of the river, at the edge of the deep hole. I peered down into the rippling water, but it was too dark to see anything. However, I knew that, with my swim mask, I would be able to see the bottom after I dove in.

"Don't worry," I said. "He probably isn't there, anyway. I'm sure that the only thing I'll see will be some fish."

Well, I'd see a few fish, all right . . . but I would also see something else.

And that something was over twelve feet long.

I took a deep breath, hesitated, and gently fell forward into the river.

The water was cold, and it took my breath away. I immediately inhaled deeply and began to breathe through my snorkel.

And below me, the bottom of the river was clearly visible. It was cool to see a completely different world . . . just by wearing a swim mask. Long, stringy, lime-colored seaweed swayed gently in the current. There were a few sunken logs, some of them obscured by the thick, wisping seaweed. A small brook trout, the size of a banana, was snuggled up close to a large rock.

The current pulled me downstream, and I had to kick my fins to remain in one place. My breath howled through the snorkel, sounding hollow and loud, even with my ears beneath the surface.

I saw another fish—a brown trout—next to a log. The fish wasn't very big.

I raised my mask out of the water, still kicking with my fins to keep pace with the current. I could see Heather on shore, squinting. One hand was raised to the bill of her baseball cap to help shield her eyes from the sun.

"See anything?" she called out.

I shook my head. "Nothing," I replied, trying to speak through the snorkel. My voice sounded weird and my words were garbled, so I pulled the snorkel out of my mouth. "Nothing, yet," I said. "Just a couple of fish and some logs. I'll keep looking."

I bit down again on the snorkel and put my head back into the water. Again, I saw weeds, logs, and rocks . . . but no alligator.

I let the current carry me a short distance downstream. The hole became deeper. In one part, it was nearly impossible to see the bottom. A mane of seaweed swirled and I flinched, because there was a long, dark, object beneath it . . . but it was only a log. It had the shape of what could have been an alligator, though, and it had freaked me out for a moment.

Then I heard a sound. Not the sound of water, but a different sound altogether. It sounded strange, and I could barely make it out. It was a high-pitched sound, all garbled and broken.

I pulled my head out of the water. Suddenly, the sound was much louder, much clearer. I snapped my head in the direction it was coming from.

It was Heather! Heather was pointing and screaming!

"Craig!" she shouted. *"Look out! Look out!"*

14

When I turned to look upstream at what she was pointing at, it was almost too late. Bearing down on me was a large aluminum canoe. Its occupants were paddling fast, and they didn't even see me swimming in the middle of the river.

There was no way I would have time to swim around the canoe and get out of its way. The only thing I would be able to do was to dive down and hope the canoe would pass overhead without hitting me.

I took the deepest breath I could and sank beneath the surface. Using my fins, I kicked myself lower, lower still, until I was sure I was deep enough.

A large, dark shadow fell over me as the canoe passed. I looked up from the bottom of the river and saw two paddles—one near the front of the canoe, the other near the back—dipping in, then out, dipping in again, then out.

Then, just as quickly as it had appeared, it was gone. The shadow vanished, and, above me, the surface shined, distorted in the bright sunlight.

That had been a close one!

I surfaced. From the shore, Heather was giving the careless canoeists an earful.

"Next time, watch where you're going!" she was shouting. "My friend was swimming in the river, and you almost hit him!"

The canoeists didn't pay any attention, and, in the next moment, they vanished around the bend.

"Are you all right?" Heather asked.

I pulled the snorkel from my mouth. "Fine," I said. "Thanks for warning me, though. If they would have hit me, that would've hurt."

"People ought to look where they're going," she said angrily.

"I'm going to keep looking for the alligator," I said. "Keep your eye out for more canoes."

"Okay," Heather said, glancing upstream.

I put the snorkel into my mouth, bit down, and placed my face in the water. The bottom of the river appeared, and I allowed myself to drift a bit further downstream. Here, it was mostly gravel and a bit of seaweed. I didn't see any fish at all.

After a few minutes of searching, I still hadn't spotted any sign of the alligator. I had allowed the current to take me downstream, down to a bend where the water became shallow. Finally, when the water was only waist deep, I stood up and took the snorkel out of my mouth.

Heather was upstream on the bank, watching me. Every few seconds she glanced upstream to make sure there were no canoes coming. She cupped her hands around her mouth. "Find anything?" she shouted.

"No," I shouted back. "Nothing at all. I guess it was just a waste of time."

It was at that very moment that I heard a splash to the right of me. At first, I thought it was a trout, feeding on a bug on the surface.

And then I saw movement and heard another splash.

But it wasn't an alligator . . . it was *two* alligators!

And one of them was headed right for me!

My mask was still over my face, and I yanked it off as I began to struggle to make it to the riverbank before the awful reptile attacked. The alligator that was heading in my direction wasn't very big—maybe about the size of a baseball bat—but it was big enough to make me want to get away from it, and pronto. Heather heard the commotion and started yelling.

"What is it, Craig?" she shouted. "What's wrong?"

"*Alligators!*" I wailed. *"Two of them! One of them is after me!"*

Which, as it turned out, wasn't the case. When I reached the shore, I turned to see the alligator swimming to the other side of the river. He had either given up chasing me, or maybe he was more frightened of me than I was of him.

Meanwhile, Heather was racing down the trail, following the stream to where I stood.

"Where is he?" she huffed, as she approached.

"Right there!" I pointed.

Across the river, the alligator had reached the bank. It scrambled up and over a log that was partially submerged in the water, and climbed onto shore. Then it vanished into the tall grass.

"Did you see it?" I asked excitedly.

"Yeah!" Heather replied. "Craig! You were right! There really *are* alligators in the AuSable!"

"I told you!" I cried. "I *knew* I didn't imagine it!"

"Where did they come from?" Heather asked.

I shook my head and pointed to the other side of the river. "I don't know," I said, "but over there is probably the best place to start looking."

Heather's mouth fell. "What do you mean?" she asked. "Craig! They're *alligators!* They'll eat us up!"

"Those two weren't that big," I said. "I think we could probably outrun them."

"You're really serious?!?!" Heather said.

"Yeah," I said. "Let's go home and get some pants on and get into our waders. I think it's really swampy on the other side of the river, so we can keep our waders on while we walk and look for the alligators."

"I think that's just asking for trouble," Heather said.

"We'll be fine," I replied. "Besides . . . I'd really like to get a picture of one of those alligators!"

Heather and I talked about it some more. Finally, she agreed to help explore the woods and swamp on the other side of the river.

It was an exploration that would lead us far back into the woods, along a curious stream, to something that we never knew existed . . . .

It didn't take us long to hike home. When I went inside to change clothes, my mom was in the living room, reading.

"What are you up to today?" she asked.

"Oh, Heather and I are going to hunt for alligators in the woods," I replied, very matter-of-factly.

Well . . . it was the truth.

Mom smiled and raised her eyebrows. "Alligators, huh?" she said.

"Yeah," I replied. "Great big ones." I stretched my arms wide.

"Well, you two have fun," Mom replied with a grin. "And if you find any alligators, don't bring them home."

"I won't," I said, and I went upstairs to change.

Heather met me at the shed. She had her waders on, but she wasn't wearing her vest. I had just stepped into my waders, fastened the suspenders, and slipped into my vest, checking the pockets to make sure that I had my camera.

"You know, I've been thinking," she said. "Maybe this isn't such a good idea. Maybe we ought to tell someone."

"I did," I said.

Heather's eyes widened, and her jaw dropped. "You did?" she said. "Who? When?"

"I told my mom, just a few minutes ago."

"What did she say?" Heather asked.

"She said for us to have fun, and not to bring any alligators home."

"She believed you?" Heather replied.

I smirked. "Of course not. I knew she wouldn't. But she asked me what I was up to today, and I told her the truth. I'm not going to lie to my mother. Are you ready?"

Heather shrugged. "As ready as I'll ever be," she answered.

We hiked back to the bend where we'd spotted the two alligators, and made our way across the river. I looked all around for alligators, but I didn't find any.

On the other side of the stream, the forest was very thick. I had never set foot on that side of the river, simply because there was no trail there. It was mostly swamp land, filled with cedar trees that grew tightly together. Long, green grass grew all the way to the river's edge, and I was pretty sure that the terrain was soft and mucky.

And it looked like the perfect place for alligators to hide.

I stepped out of the stream and into the waist-high green grass. Then I turned, grabbed Heather's hand, and helped her out of the river.

The day was hot, and I was sweating in my waders and vest. The sun was bright, and I wished I had brought my sunglasses.

"See anything?" Heather asked, as we peered through the trees and tangled branches. It was shady and dark, and I was hoping that it would be a little cooler in the swamp.

"Not yet," I replied. "Come on."

As we hiked through the tall grass, ducking under limbs, our waders sank up to our ankles in thick, chocolate-colored mud.

"It will be hard to find any alligators in this stuff," Heather said, as we struggled through the swamp. "It's so thick, they could hide in the grass and we'd never see them."

Mosquitos buzzed around our heads, and I swatted at them with my hand. I stopped to push a branch out of the way, and it was then that I saw it.

A stream.

It wasn't very big—maybe a foot wide—and it was very dark. It looked like a thin black snake winding through the bright green grass. There are a lot of small creeks like that along the AuSable. They're called 'feeder streams', and they come from a spring or a lake or pond, and drain into the river.

We walked through the grass until we reached the tiny stream. It was only a few inches deep, but the dark, silty mud made it look much deeper. When I stepped into it, I sank up to my knee in mud!

"Man, this is like quicksand," I said, struggling to pull my leg out. "Let's not get stuck in this stuff."

"Let's follow it and see where it goes," Heather said.

"That's what I was thinking," I agreed, and we made our way though the tall grass, following the stream through the forest.

After only a few minutes of walking, we were deep in the swamp. The trees grew even thicker, and the air was heavy and damp.

Suddenly, Heather grabbed my arm.

"Craig! Look!"

She pointed.

Not far away, near the tiny creek, the grass was moving. Not from wind or a breeze, but from something else. Something was pushing the grass . . . and I knew exactly what it was.

An alligator.

And by the look of how much grass was moving, it would be bigger than any of the alligators that we'd seen so far.

17

We didn't move an inch. A mosquito landed on my neck, but I didn't move to swat it. I was too focused on the rustling grass ahead of us. The alligator was going to appear any moment, I was sure.

Then, the grass stopped moving.

Heather and I waited, motionless, watching the still grass.

It rustled again.

Suddenly, a dark snout appeared. As we watched, it grew larger as the grass fell away.

"That's not an alligator!" Heather exclaimed. "That's a snapping turtle! And he's *gigantic!*"

On one hand, I was disappointed that it wasn't an alligator. But, on the other hand, it was cool to see the turtle. Heather was right: it was gigantic. I'd heard that snapping turtles in Michigan can get big—almost the size of a washtub—and weigh up to thirty-five pounds! But I'd never seen one that big . . . until now.

We trudged through the muck and grass until we were only a few feet from the turtle. He was as big around as a beach ball, and his shell was black and splotched with dark green moss.

"He's cool," Heather said.

"Maybe he's a she," I said.

"She's cool, then," Heather said.

The turtle drew its head back into its shell. We were careful not to get too close. I've caught some small snapping turtles, and once they grab onto something with their jaws, they don't let go very easily. I sure didn't want a giant snapper latching onto my leg!

"Well, let's leave him or her alone," I said, "and keep looking for alligators."

I took two steps forward . . . and found exactly what we were looking for.

Heather saw it first. She gripped my arm and pointed. "Look!" she exclaimed. "That's no turtle!"

And it wasn't!

She was pointing at a pair of eyes and a small snout that were barely visible above the surface of the dark creek. It was an alligator, all right . . . but it was a small one . . . only about a foot long. If we hadn't been paying attention, we might have walked right by it.

"I should have brought a net and a big can!" I said. "Then, we could have caught it!"

Just as I spoke, the small alligator dunked beneath the surface. It turned and began swimming away, heading up the thin, winding creek.

"Come on," I said. "Let's follow it!"

We waded through the grass and mud, trying to keep up with the retreating alligator. He moved fast in the water, and it was hard to keep pace. When it stopped and surfaced, we stopped, too, not wanting to get too close. I reached into my vest and pulled out my camera.

"There," I said, as I clicked off a couple of pictures. "Now we'll have proof!"

"But that still doesn't answer the question," Heather said.

"What question?" I asked.

"What are alligators doing around here?" she asked. "I mean . . . you caught one on a fly a couple of nights ago. Then we saw two in the river, earlier today. And now, this little one, here in the creek. Where did they come from, and how many more are there?"

We were about to get our answer.

I looked around, and noticed something peculiar.

No sounds.

None. At all.

Like the other night, when I'd been fishing, all sounds stopped . . . right before I caught the alligator. I hadn't remembered it until this very moment.

And that's when I noticed something else.

Eyes. Several pairs of dark, glassy eyes were staring at us. I could make out long snouts, camouflaged in the thick weeds and brush. We hadn't noticed them before because they seemed to blend right into their surroundings. And, judging by the size of their eyes and snouts, these alligators weren't little.

But there was no mistaking it.

At that moment, we were being watched—

By real, live alligators!

Wearing my waders and vest made my skin clammy and hot . . . but a cold trickle of fear iced down my back, creeping all through my body. I couldn't move. I could only stare at those cold, penetrating eyes, glaring back at us.

But the alligators hadn't moved, either.

Yet.

But what if they did? What if they attacked us? Some of the alligators I've seen on television move pretty fast. Not the little ones, of course. But the big ones can really move.

And we didn't know exactly how big they were, because they were all hidden so well. But we could see their eyes and their snouts, and it was easy to see that the alligators around us were bigger than the ones we'd seen so far.

For the time being, there was nothing we could do. I knew that if the alligators wanted to attack us, they would.

So, we just stood there, Heather and I, not moving, not speaking.

Then—

One of the alligators moved.

It turned its head, looking left to right.

Then it began to crawl forward, toward the stream, which had now grown to about the width of a car. The alligator slunk through the weeds and slipped into the water, and I could see, for the first time, how big it was.

It was almost as big as me!

As we watched, the other alligators also crawled forward. I counted five of them, all about the same size. They all slipped into the stream and began swimming away.

"Craig!" Heather whispered. *"Your camera! Your camera!"*

I had been so scared that I'd forgotten all about the camera in my vest. I quickly pulled it out and held the viewfinder up to my eye, but it was too late. The alligators were gone.

"Let's follow them!" I said. "I've got to get a picture!"

"You are out of your mind!" Heather said. "I am *not* following those things! We should go to the police or something!"

"We will!" I insisted. "But those alligators are coming from *somewhere,* and I want to know *where!"*

"You already talked me into coming this far," Heather said, "but you're not going to talk me into going any farther."

"Let's just follow the stream a little ways and see where it goes," I pleaded. "We have to find out where those alligators are coming from!"

After some more talking, I was able to persuade Heather to come with me. I promised her that we wouldn't go far.

So, we continued on, following the creek as it wound through the swamp. After a while the trees thinned out a bit, and it wasn't so marshy. But there were still a lot of trees, and it was slow going.

"This creek probably leads to a giant alligator pond filled with giant alligators," Heather said.

I laughed. "I doubt that," I replied.

I shouldn't have doubted. In fact, I should have listened to Heather.

But I didn't. The two of us trudged on in our waders, ignoring the heat and the mosquitos, cautiously on the lookout for alligators that might be hiding in the woods or near the stream.

Unfortunately, alligators can hide a lot better than I thought.

Suddenly, there was a splash in the water behind us. Heather and I turned . . . just in time to see the horrible reptile coming right for us!

The alligator was heading upstream, swimming toward us.

"Run!" I shouted.

"In waders?!?!" Heather exclaimed.

"We don't have any choice!" I said, as I turned and began to run. I pushed branches out of the way. "Let's go into the woods, and stay away from the creek! The alligator can move faster in the water than on land!"

"How do you know?!?!" Heather panted.

"I think I saw it on TV once!" I said. "Let's just keep out of its way!"

Running while wearing waders isn't easy. They're bulky, and they don't allow you to move your legs very fast.

Plus, we were in the woods, which made it even harder. We had to run around trees, over logs and stumps, and push branches out of the way.

The good thing was, when I turned around, there was no sign of the alligator. I don't know if he had been after us or not, and I didn't care. I just wanted to get away from him. The bad thing, however, was that I'd been too frightened to take the time to snap a picture.

"I think we're far enough away," I said, as I stopped to catch my breath. My chest heaved. Sweat beaded on my forehead, and a tiny trickle ran down my nose. I wiped it away with my hand. I was breathing heavy, and my shirt was clammy and hot beneath my vest.

"That one was big!" Heather gasped. Her eyes scanned the woods nervously, as if there might be another alligator hiding close by at that very moment. We looked around and listened for any movement, but we didn't see or hear anything except the normal sounds of the forest, and the thin hum of a few cars in the distance.

"You know," I said, "I think I know where we are."

"Yeah, so do I," Heather said. "We're in the woods."

"No, I mean I think I know *where* we are in the forest," I replied. "I think we're near the old fish hatchery on North Down River Road."

"What's that?" Heather asked.

"Oh, it's kind of like a trout farm. They used to raise fish and use them to stock rivers and lakes. There are some big ponds there, made out of cement. When it was open, you could go and feed the fish. There is a big, old building there, too, but it's not used anymore. In fact—"

I paused and looked around. Then I pointed.

"—the sun is over there, and the car sounds are coming from over there, so, if I'm right, the fish hatchery is over there, in that direction."

"But that's the direction of the stream that we were following," Heather said.

I nodded. "Something really weird is going on," I said.

"We already knew that," Heather said. "Alligators don't belong in Michigan."

"Yeah, but there's more to it than that," I said. "If that creek flows from the fish hatchery, then that's where the alligators were headed."

"So, what does that mean?" Heather asked.

"That's what we're going to find out," I replied.

Oh, we'd find out all right . . . but, at the time, we had no idea how terrifying the truth would be.

21

We hiked back to the creek, keeping our eyes out for more alligators. We didn't see any.

"Come on," I said, turning when we reached the small stream. "The old fish hatchery should be this way."

Although walking through the woods with waders on was hot and tiring, I was glad I was wearing them. The ground next to the creek was often muddy, soft, and wet, and I would have ruined my shoes for sure. With waders on, it didn't matter how swampy the terrain was, because my feet and legs were protected.

We didn't have to walk far. Just as I suspected, the stream flowed from the old fish hatchery. However, there was a chain link fence that crossed the stream, preventing us from going any farther. In fact, it looked like the fence went around the entire perimeter of the property. On the other side of the fence was the hatchery. We could see the old building in the distance, and some of the long, rectangular cement pools where the fish used to be kept. No one was around.

"That's strange," Heather said. "If the alligators swam upstream this far, where did they go?"

We were standing in the creek, in water up to our knees. The fence was right in front of us. Not only did it prevent us from going any farther, but the fence went all the way down to the bottom of the stream, meaning that nothing could get in or out . . . unless it was small enough to slip through the fence. A small alligator might be able to make it through, but certainly not a bigger one.

I glanced around, wary that there might be an alligator close by, watching us at that very instant.

Heather looked around, too. "Well," she said, her voice trembling, "if the alligators aren't in there, that must mean that they're out here somewhere."

"No," I said, shaking my head. "That doesn't make sense. All of the alligators we saw were headed this way, like they were going someplace."

"Well, there's no way they went though this," Heather said, fingering the fence.

I looked to the left, along the fence line. Then, I looked to the right.

Heather is right, I thought. *The bigger alligators would never be able to make it through this fence. Not unless . . . .*

I stepped out of the creek, took a few steps along the fence . . . and got my answer.

"Heather!" I exclaimed, as I knelt down. "Come here and look at this!"

Heather stepped out of the stream to join me.

"What?" she asked. "What did you find?"

I pointed.

Where the fence met the ground was a large hole that had been dug. There was a gaping space beneath the fence. There were claw marks in the dirt, and I could only assume they were from alligators.

"They dug a hole beneath the fence!" Heather exclaimed. "That's how the alligators got out!"

Suddenly, we heard the sounds of movement behind us. Branches snapped. Twigs broke.

And we heard something I will never forget as long as I live.

A loud, vicious snarl.

A snapping of powerful jaws.

A clenching of sharp teeth.

We turned . . . only to face a monster.

22

Heather screamed as the giant beast lunged. She sprang to the left and I darted to the right, frantically pushing bushes and branches out of the way. The alligator crashed through the brush, but I didn't turn around to see how close he was to me. I just wanted to get away . . . and fast!

The chain link fence rattled and shook. Heather screamed again as I splashed into the creek.

I stopped and turned.

Heather was nowhere in sight, but I could see the big alligator struggling beneath the fence. It slipped under and wriggled to the other side, where it quickly fled to one of the trout ponds. The beast splashed into the water, and vanished.

"Heather!" I shouted, lunging out of the creek and into the brush. "Are you all right?!?!"

"I'm here!" she said. "I'm okay!"

Branches moved and shook, and Heather emerged. She had a small scratch on her cheek from a tree branch, but, other than that, she was unhurt.

"I got away just in time!" she said. "That thing tried to bite me. Look!" She stuck out her right leg, displaying a three-inch gash in her waders.

"Did he get you?!?!" I asked.

Heather shook her head. "He missed," she said. "He only got my waders. They're ruined."

"Better your waders than you," I said, gazing at the rip in Heather's waders.

"Let's go home," I said. "I don't know what's going on, but it's too dangerous to stay around here. We've got to tell somebody about—"

I was interrupted by another snarl.

And another one.

Branches cracked, and brush seemed to be moving all around us. Heather and I backed up against the fence. We couldn't see anything except the rustling of grass and shrubs.

And then—

There they were.

Alligators.

Not one or two, but *three* of them.

One alligator was bad enough. Two were terrible.

Three of them . . . well, that was a *catastrophe*.

But worst of all, Heather and I were backed against the fence. The alligators had surrounded us, and we had no place to go.

This time, we weren't getting away.

My palms pressed flat against the fence behind us, and my fingers coiled around the wires. I thought about trying to climb up, but it would be impossible wearing waders. Besides . . . even if we were able to climb the fence, the alligators still might be able to get at us.

The alligator on the left lunged at Heather, and she screamed. However, the reptile backed off, hissing and snorting. They were like a pack of angry dogs, circling their prey.

Behind Heather, on the other side of the fence, was a big log. It was cut in several pieces, each of which were about three feet long.

And that gave me an idea.

"Heather!" I shouted. *"Climb under the fence!"*

"What?!?!" she back. *"Are you crazy?!?! There are alligators over there, too!"*

One of the alligators snapped its jaws and took a step forward. *"Hurry!"* I shouted. *"Just do it!"*

Heather fell to her stomach and squirmed under the fence. Even wearing her waders, it only took her a moment. Then she was on the other side, where she quickly scrambled to her feet and brushed the dirt from her shirt and waders.

I was next. I dropped down on my stomach and wriggled under the fence. Or, I *tried* to, anyway. Problem was, with my waders and my vest, I was too big to fit!

"Hurry, Craig, hurry!" Heather screeched. *"They're getting closer!"*

I struggled and squirmed. Heather grabbed one of my hands and began to pull, but it was no use.

If I were only a little smaller, I could probably make it. But with my waders and my vest, I was out of luck.

Meanwhile, the alligators seemed to be getting angrier by the moment. I could hear them snapping their jaws, and I knew that they were inching closer. It was only a matter of time before they reached me and—

No, Craig! I told myself. *Don't even think about it!*

I pulled back from the hole, got on my knees, and took my fly fishing vest off as quickly as I could. Then I threw it over the fence to where Heather was standing, dropped down onto my back, and squirmed beneath the fence. All the while, the angry alligators hissed, snarled, and snapped.

"Craig!" Heather repeated. *"Hurry!"*

"Grab my hands and pull!" I shouted.

Without my vest, I was able to slip under the fence a little easier. But it was still a struggle with my waders.

Suddenly, the biggest alligator lunged forward, snapping his jaws and snarling.

"Watch out!" Heather wailed.

I swung my foot and bopped the alligator in the snout, deflecting his attack. The reptile backed off, but I knew that a simple kick wasn't going to stop him for long.

I was still struggling and squirming, trying to make it to the other side of the fence. Suddenly . . . the alligator struck again.

This time, I wasn't fast enough. The vicious beast surged forward, jaws open. I could see rows of razor sharp teeth, and I tried to pull my leg away . . . but it was too late. The huge alligator clamped down on my right foot, and I knew it was the end of the line.

I was about to become alligator food.

I kicked and thrashed like crazy. The alligator's teeth hadn't punctured my heavy rubber boots, but I knew that it was only a matter of time.

"Pull, Heather, pull!" I screamed.

"I'm pulling as hard as I can!" she shouted back.

I felt like I was a human dog toy, in a dangerous game of tug-of-war. Heather was pulling my hands, and an alligator was pulling my foot!

I mustered up all the strength that I had, and yanked my leg with all my might. The alligator lost its grip.

I was free!

But I wouldn't be for long, if I didn't act fast.

I quickly pulled my legs from beneath the fence, rolled over onto my stomach, and scrambled to my feet.

"The logs!" I shouted, pointing. *"Let's bring a log over, so the alligators can't get beneath the fence!"*

We darted to one of the cut logs. It was about three feet long, and far too heavy for us to lift. Instead, we rolled it using the palms of our hands.

At the hole in the fence, the three alligators were all trying to get through at the same time. The hole wasn't big enough, of course, and that gave us the time we needed to roll the heavy log over the hole, blocking their way.

"Let's get another log, just in case!" I said, and we quickly rolled another log up against the one that covered the hole.

On the other side of the fence, the alligators were trying to push the log with their snouts, but they weren't strong enough. We were safe . . . at least for the time being.

We looked around. The grounds of the fish hatchery were large. Before us, there were several long, rectangular pools made of cement. They looked like bowling alleys filled with water. There were also cement sidewalks that wound around the pools and throughout the grounds. On the far side, a large, old, two-story building sat. It was weathered and aged, and its white paint was chipping and flaking off.

"Let's get out of here," I said.

"That's the best idea I've heard all day," Heather replied. "I don't care where the alligators came from. I just want to go home."

I did, too. I mean . . . it was kind of cool to see alligators, but this whole thing had become far too dangerous.

"The main gate is over that way," I said, pointing. "Let's go. We can walk into town and call my dad. Man . . . is he going to freak when I tell him about the alligators!"

I picked up my vest and slipped it on. Then we walked along the fence, heading for the main gate. Behind us, the three alligators were still struggling to push the logs, without much success. But I knew it was only a matter of time before they started to dig another hole. By then, I wanted to be long gone.

When we got to the main gate, however, we were in for a surprise:

It was locked!

There was a chain wrapped around the gate, bound together with a big, steel padlock.

"We're not getting out this way," I said.

Heather and I turned and looked around.

"Wait!" Heather said, thrusting her arm out. She was pointing at the old hatchery building.

A man was going inside!

"Hey!" I shouted, waving my hands. "Mister! Hey, Mister!"

The man didn't hear me, as he had already entered through the big main door and closed it.

"Come on!" I said. "He'll be able to let us out of here, I bet! And he probably knows where the alligators came from!"

We started running, and I thought about the questions I would ask the man.

Where did the alligators come from? How come they seem to be drawn to the old fish hatchery? How many are there?

Oh, I'd get my answers soon enough, and our adventure would soon be over . . . but that's when our nightmare would begin.

25

Heather and I ran around the cement ponds. I was a little wary as I glanced into the dark, still waters, as we'd seen an alligator go into one of the ponds just a short while ago. I kept waiting for one to leap from the water and attack us, but it didn't. In fact, we didn't see any alligators at all.

Soon, we were bounding up to the front door of the old hatchery building. I raised my fist and gave the door three hard knocks.

We waited, our lungs heaving.

I knocked again.

No answer.

"Maybe he's gone," Heather said.

I shook my head. "No," I replied. "We saw him only a few moments ago. We would have seen him leave. He's got to be here. But the building is so big that he might not hear us knocking."

"Is there another door?" Heather asked.

I shrugged. "One way to find out," I said. "Come on. Lets go around to the back of the building."

We darted around the building. The wood was old, and the gray paint was peeling off. In some places, the wood was rotting away.

We rounded the corner to the back of the building. Sure enough, there was a back door.

And not only was it unlocked . . . it was partially open!

I pulled it open farther. "Hello?" I shouted. My voice echoed down a long, empty hallway. "Anybody home? Hello?"

No answer.

"Anybody home?" I called out again, even louder this time.

There was still no response. We listened, but we didn't hear anything. The only sounds were the hum of cars on the distant road.

I stepped inside.

"What are you doing?" Heather hissed.

"Don't worry," I said. "We're not doing anything wrong. We just need to find that guy so he can let us out of here."

Reluctantly, Heather followed me inside.

We found ourselves in a long hallway. There were no lights, and the air was dry and stale. Like the outside of the building, paint was chipping from the walls. Small piles of gray-white flecks were on the floor.

"It doesn't look like anyone has been here in a hundred years," Heather said, as she looked around.

We passed a number of rooms as we walked. All of them were dark and empty.

"This place would make a good haunted house," I said.

"Don't say that," Heather said. "I don't like haunted houses. And I don't like alligators, either."

"Anybody home?" I called out as we walked.

At the end of the hall was a staircase that led down. The old boards creaked and groaned as we followed them down to the lower level.

"It's another hallway," I said, as we reached the bottom of the stairs.

It was darker than the hallway upstairs, but one thing was very clear: at the far end of the hall was a thin band of light coming from beneath one of the doors!

"That's where he is!" I said. "Come on!"

We raced down the hall, our footsteps echoing along the old, bare walls. It only took us a few seconds to make it to the end of the hallway.

I stopped at the door and knocked. However, the door was open a tiny bit, and it moved under the pressure of my fist. Slowly, the door opened, farther and farther, until it was all the way open.

I stared.

Heather stared.

There's a saying that goes like this:

Seeing is believing.

Well, we knew what we were seeing . . . we just couldn't *believe* it.

An alligator farm.

That's what it was.

Impossible, I know. But the room was huge! It was filled with tables and large aquariums and pens.

And there were alligators everywhere! They were all safely contained, but there were dozens of them! Some were just babies, about a foot long. Others were bigger, nearly three or four feet long! This was where the alligators were coming from!

"Wow," I said, my voice barely a whisper. "What is going on here? Why would someone have an alligator farm in an old fish hatchery?"

Heather shook her head. She didn't say anything.

By this time, I was getting warm in my vest and waders. I slipped my vest off, unhooked my suspenders, and stepped out of the waders. Heather did the same.

Carrying our waders, we walked around the room. It was filled with aquariums that contained alligators of all sizes. Some of them were different shades of brown, but, for the most part, all the alligators looked the same. Some of them were hissing and snarling, their jaws opening and closing. Even the small ones looked ferocious, with tiny, sharp teeth.

"Somebody is raising these things here," Heather said.

"Yeah, but why?" I wondered aloud. "Alligators shouldn't be in the AuSable River. They'll eat all the trout and scare all of the fishermen and canoeists. They might even attack people."

But then I had another thought.

What if we aren't supposed to be here? What if this place is supposed to be secret?

Then, we'd be in trouble.

And that's when we heard footsteps coming from outside in the hall. They were far off, but they were coming closer.

We had to make a decision, and fast. Should we wait until whoever it was showed up, or should we try to hide and not be found out? After all, if this place was supposed to be a secret, the man—or whoever it was—might be angry with us.

I made a decision.

"Someone's coming!" I hissed. *"Let's hide!"*

"What are you talking about?!?!" Heather demanded in a whisper. *"We came here to find the guy we saw outside. Now you want to hide from him?"*

"Let's hide, just in case we aren't supposed to be here!" I said.

My eyes darted around the room, looking for a hiding place. All the while, the sound of footsteps grew louder and louder.

"Over there," I said. *"Under that table. Come on!"*

It wasn't the best place to hide, but I didn't see a closet or anything else that would keep us out of sight. The table on the other side of the room would at least give us some cover. After all . . . the room was filled with tables. It would be difficult to see us, unless the man walked right by the table where we were hiding.

We darted between two rows of tables that had aquariums containing a few small alligators. The reptiles hissed at us as we passed, but we ignored them.

"Hurry!" I said. Still carrying our waders, we ducked down and scrambled beneath the table, crouched low, and waited.

The footsteps stopped at the door, and we heard a cold, angry voice.

"All right!" the man growled. "I know you're here! You might as well come out now! There is no other way out!"

Gulp!

I didn't know what to do.

Here we were, in the lower level of the old Grayling fish hatchery, hiding in what only could be an alligator farm.

And we'd been found out!

We had no choice but to obey.

Leaving my waders and vest, I climbed out from beneath the table and stood up. Heather did the same. We were shaking and trembling all over.

On the other side of the room stood the man that we'd seen entering the building. He was wearing light brown pants and a green shirt. His hair was dark, and he had a thick mustache. He looked like he was about as old as my dad.

He raised his hand, and, with a single finger, motioned us to come toward him. My legs felt like rubber as we made our way through the rows of tables and aquariums. Alligators hissed at us.

By the time we reached the other side of the room, the man had his arms crossed. He was frowning, and he looked angry.

"Do you mind telling me just what you two are doing in here?" he asked.

"I . . . uh . . . um . . . we . . . we were trying to figure out wh . . . where the alligators were coming from," I stammered. It was hard to get my words out because I was so scared.

"Ah," the man said. "And how did you know that there were alligators here?"

"The river," I said. "We . . . we saw them in the AuSable River, and we followed them here."

"Impossible," the man grunted. "Now, tell me the truth."

"That *is* the truth," Heather said. "We saw alligators in the river, and we followed them up a creek that led here."

"All of the alligators are contained in the hatchery," the man insisted. "There is no way for them to escape."

"Yes, there is," I said, nodding. "They dug a hole underneath the fence. We can take you there and show you."

"That won't be necessary," the man said. "Besides . . . it's feeding time for the alligators. I'm busy, and so are you two."

"You . . . you mean we can leave?" Heather asked.

The man laughed. "Leave?!?! Of course not. Why, you're going to be our dinner guests!"

"Dinner guests?" I asked.

"Of course," the man said with a sly smile. "My alligators just *love* children."

Oh, no!

All the blood drained from my face. I was so scared that I could actually feel my skin tingling. I felt dizzy.

Heather's hands flew to her face, covering her mouth to stifle a scream.

The man must have sensed how frightened we were, because he laughed and shook his head.

"Hey, come on," he chuckled. "I'm only kidding. It was just a joke, and not a very good one. Sorry to scare you like that."

That was a relief! My dizziness faded.

"I was only kidding," the man continued. "It's time to feed the alligators. I thought you might want to watch."

"Sure," I said. "But . . . what is this place? An alligator farm?"

"Exactly," the man said. "I'm raising alligators here, but, unfortunately, it's not going as well as planned."

"Why here?" Heather asked. "I mean . . . alligators don't belong in Michigan."

"That's exactly why I thought it would be unique," the man said, and he continued to explain what he had been working on.

He said his name was Mr. Garton, and he was a herpetologist, which is someone who studies reptiles and amphibians. He said he wanted to use the old fish hatchery to create an alligator farm as a tourist attraction. His hope was that people would flock to his alligator farm to see the alligators, since there was no other place in Michigan where you could see them, except in zoos.

"But," he continued, "things haven't worked out like I had planned. A couple of the alligators have gotten way too big, and there's no way we can keep them in the ponds of the hatchery. Especially Buttons. He's gotten huge."

Heather and I looked at each other.

"Buttons?" we both said in unison.

"Yeah," Mr. Garton replied with a nod. "Buttons is over seven feet long. I never expected any of my alligators to get that big."

Heather giggled, and I did, too.

"What's so funny?" Mr. Garton asked.

"'Buttons' seems like a funny name for an alligator," Heather said.

"Yeah," I said. "How come you didn't call him 'Fang' or something?"

"Well, I named him that because when he was little, he was cute as a button."

I giggled a little bit more. The thought of a giant alligator named 'Buttons' was still pretty funny.

"Do you want to see him?" Mr. Garton asked. "I keep him in another room, all by himself. I made a special door that he can go in and out of when I open it for him. He's very vicious and doesn't like people, but he's no danger, as long as he's in the room I built for him. He might be sleeping now, but you can still see him."

I looked at Heather, and she looked back at me.

"Sure," I said. "That would be cool."

We followed Mr. Garton out of the room and down the hall.

"You see," he continued explaining, "I thought that my alligator farm would be a fun tourist attraction. However, I've realized that it's not going to work. The winters are going to be too cold, even if we kept them in the building. Plus, some of them have been able to escape from the cement ponds and run loose over the grounds. If there were tourists walking around, they would be in danger."

"What are you going to do with all of the alligators?" Heather asked.

"I'm giving them to some zoos, where they'll all have a good home. I'm going to miss a few of them, though. They've sort of become friends."

"And what about the fish hatchery?" I asked. "What's going to happen to this place?"

"A local group is going to turn it back into a fish hatchery and raise trout," he said, "like it was meant to be. They even plan to fix up this old building, and make it like new again. People will be able to come and experience a real fish hatchery."

That sounded cool. I've seen pictures of what the fish hatchery looked like a long time ago, and it would be neat to see it open again.

"Here we are," Mr. Garton said, and he pushed open a door.

He stopped. A confused look came over his face. Then he looked completely horrified.

"What's the matter?" I asked.

"Buttons!" he cried. "Buttons is gone! He tore out the door with his teeth and claws!"

Just when I thought that the whole mystery had been solved, that we were going to make it home safely, we had another problem to deal with.

A giant, man-eating alligator was on the loose!

The look on Mr. Garton's face told us more than we needed to know.

He was *terrified*.

"He was just here twenty minutes ago!" he exclaimed. "I checked on him, and he was fine!"

Heather and I looked around the room, which actually looked more like a pen . . . the kind you might see at a zoo. There were several large logs and tree branches near one wall. The entire floor was covered with sand, and there was a long pool of water that was about a foot deep.

However, on the far side of the pen, a small wooden door had been ripped apart. There were scratches and bite marks on the walls around it.

"This is going to be dangerous," Mr. Garton said. "I'm going to need you two to stay in this building while I find Buttons and try to get him back into his pen. The good thing is, he can't go far."

"Oh, yes he can," I said, nodding. "Alligators have dug a hole under the fence on the other side of the hatchery."

"That's how we knew to come here," Heather said. "Like we told you before . . . some of the alligators have gotten loose."

Mr. Garton shook his head in despair. "I didn't think it was possible. I thought that we'd done everything we could to make sure the alligators couldn't get out."

"Well, we know of at least three of them that are on the other side of the fence," I said. "That's how we got in here. We had to crawl under the fence to get away from three alligators."

"All right, then," Mr. Garton said, "here's what we're going to do. I'm going to go out and see if I can find Buttons. You two stay in here."

"Are you going to be all right?" I asked.

Mr. Garton nodded. "Buttons will recognize me. He'll know that I won't harm him. I'll take a fish with me—he loves fish—and maybe I can get him to crawl back into his pen."

"But what about the other alligators?" Heather asked. "Aren't there other alligators out there?"

"Yes," Mr. Garton replied. "But they usually don't leave their pools. I won't have to worry about them."

We followed Mr. Garton as he led us to yet another door. When he opened it, we could see a row of freezers.

"This is where we keep the fish," he said. "Usually, the alligators don't like the fish right out of the freezer, but we don't have time to thaw any out."

He opened one of the freezer doors and pulled out two good-sized fish. They were frozen and covered with frost. Then he closed the freezer and we followed him down the hall and to the front door. He opened it and looked around.

"Where is that hole under the fence?" he asked.

I pointed to the other side of the hatchery. "Over there, just a few feet from the stream."

"I'll go there first," he said, "just to make sure that Buttons hasn't gotten out."

"We put two big logs at the hole," Heather said, "so he would have to push them out of his way."

"I'm going to close the door behind me," Mr. Garton said. "You'll be safe inside. I'll be back in a few minutes."

"Wait," I said. I knew that I should call home and let my mom and dad know where we were and what was going on. "Do you have a phone?" I asked.

Mr. Garton shook his head. "We don't have phone service here at the hatchery, yet," he said. "And my cellular phone has a dead battery."

I shrugged. "That's okay," I said. I would just have to wait a little while before I called home.

"Be careful," Heather cautioned, and Mr. Garton nodded. Then he closed the door.

"Let's watch through that window," I said, and we walked over to a big window that faced the hatchery grounds. From there, we had a big, wide view of most of the hatchery.

Mr. Garton, a fish in each hand, walked between the ponds, slowly making his way to the other side of the hatchery to see if the logs were still covering the hole beneath the fence.

He wasn't going to make it.

While we watched, we saw a movement in one of the pools. Mr. Garton had already passed by, so he couldn't see it.

But there was no mistaking what it was. Even from where we were watching, we could see the two big eyes and the snout emerge from the water. Beneath the surface, we could see the huge shadow of a gigantic alligator.

Buttons.

"Mr. Garton!" I shrieked. "Buttons is right behind you!"

Mr. Garton kept walking. He couldn't hear me!

"Let's go to the door!" Heather shouted. "He'll be able to hear us from there!"

But it was too late. Before we even had a chance to leave the window, the huge alligator was in full attack mode.

Its jaw was open.

It was moving faster.

Mr. Garton was still walking toward the fence, and he didn't see the massive beast creeping up on him.

The poor man wasn't even going to have a fighting chance.

We raced to the front door and flung it open.

"Mr. Garton!" I yelled. "Buttons is right behind you!"

Mr. Garton stopped and turned. When he saw the huge alligator climbing out of the cement pond, he froze.

"It's okay!" Mr. Garton shouted back. "He knows me. He only wants the fish!"

Mr. Garton held up one of the fish for the alligator to see. The alligator stopped, his mouth wide open. Mr. Garton threw the fish, and the alligator snapped it out of midair and swallowed it in one big gulp! I don't think the creature even took the time to chew it!

"Well, at least we know that Buttons hasn't escaped from the hatchery," Heather said.

I laughed. I still thought it was funny that an alligator would have the name 'Buttons'.

Mr. Garton began walking, making a wide circle around the big alligator. The creature turned, eyeing the man suspiciously. If Buttons was a friend of Mr. Garton's, you sure wouldn't know it by the look in his eyes. Buttons was looking at Mr. Garton like he was a fish, and was about to gobble him up.

Then, the alligator began to follow Mr. Garton. Its mouth was open, baring long, sharp teeth . . . but the beast didn't look like it was going to attack. Mr. Garton began walking backwards, holding out the remaining fish for the alligator to see. He waved it back and forth, coaxing the alligator.

"Come on, Buttons," he was saying. "Come on, buddy. That's it, come on."

"I'm sure glad he knows what he's doing," I said. "I wouldn't go out there in a million years."

Suddenly, Mr. Garton stumbled. He had been walking backwards, and he tripped on the corner of the sidewalk. Backwards he tumbled, out of control, one arm spinning madly, the other holding onto the fish. He landed flat on his back in the grass.

The fish fell from his hand.

Mr. Garton didn't move.

"Oh, no!" Heather gasped. "Mr. Garton is hurt!"

Not only was Mr. Garton hurt, but Buttons the giant alligator was coming toward him, jaws open, teeth bared.

And I knew what I had to do, even though I had just told Heather that I wouldn't go out there in a million years.

Well, it looked like my million years was up. If we wanted to save Mr. Garton, I would have to go outside.

"We've got to help him!" I told Heather.

"What?!?!" she replied. "How?"

"I have a plan!" I said, "but you'll have to help me! Come on!"

Actually, I *did* have a plan. I didn't know if it would work or not . . . but there was nothing else we could do.

Here's what my plan was:

Heather and I would get as many frozen fish as we could. Then, I would carry them outside and toss them to Buttons. Hopefully, I wouldn't have to get too close, and I could slowly lead him away from Mr. Garton.

But we'd have to hurry.

I explained to Heather what I wanted to do. She thought I was crazy, but she also knew that we really didn't have any other choice.

We raced to the freezer room and pulled out a mess of fish. I carried ten of them in my arms, and so did Heather. She wasn't too thrilled about getting fish all over her shirt, even if they were frozen.

We raced back to the front of the building. Mr. Garton was still laying on his back, motionless. We knew that he'd really hurt himself during his fall, and he needed help.

But what he really needed at the moment was for the alligator to go away! Buttons had just finished gobbling up the fish that Mr. Garton had dropped, and now he was eyeing Mr. Garton. I knew I'd have to hurry.

"When I lead Buttons away from Mr. Garton, you run out there and help him," I ordered Heather. "Leave the fish by the door, and you stay inside until the alligator is gone. If I need more fish, I'll come back and get them."

"But what if something happens to you, Craig? Then what?"

"I'll be all right," I said. "Just help Mr. Garton."

Then I turned, carrying the frozen fish, and started running across the grounds of the hatchery.

"Buttons!" I shouted, trying to attract the attention of the huge alligator. "Here, boy! Here Buttons!"

I felt silly, calling to an alligator the way someone would call to a dog.

But it worked!

The alligator saw me running, and turned. I slowed and held up a fish for the reptile to see. Then I waved it around, just like Mr. Garton had done.

Slowly, the huge alligator began coming toward me. I threw a fish, and it landed a few feet from the reptile. Buttons crawled over to it, sniffed, and then snapped the fish up. Again, it looked like he gobbled the whole thing down without even chewing!

Now, however, he was hungry for more, but I was ready. I backed up a few feet and threw another fish, careful to make sure it would land a few feet in front of the creature, leading it away from Mr. Garton.

When the alligator was almost done eating the fish, I tossed another one, leading him farther and farther from Mr. Garton. Then I turned to look at Heather. She was standing by the big front doors of the old hatchery building, ready to sprint across the yard.

"Almost ready!" I shouted to her. "Let me get Buttons just a little farther away!"

I tossed another fish. By now, the alligator was a few car lengths from Mr. Garton, who was still motionless on the ground.

"Okay!" I shouted to Heather. "Go!"

Heather started to run. However, at that very same moment, Mr. Garton leapt to his feet!

"Go back!" he shouted. "I'm fine!"

Heather turned and ran back into the hatchery building. Mr. Garton ran up to me.

"I thought you were hurt!" I said.

Mr. Garton shook his head. "I was only playing dead, in hopes that the alligator would just leave me alone. I couldn't even yell to you, because

Buttons would have known that I was alive! You helped by leading him away. Great job!"

He took the remaining fish from my arms.

"I'll use these to lure him back to his pen," he said. "He won't be causing us any more trouble."

Well, maybe Buttons wouldn't be causing us any more trouble . . . but there were other alligators still around. Sure, they weren't as big as Buttons was . . . but there were *more* of them.

And they could move faster than Buttons.

We didn't know it, of course, but at that very moment, those alligators were waiting . . . for the perfect opportunity to attack.

Their wait was almost over.

Mr. Garton led Buttons back to his pen by leaving a trail of fish that went right up to the door . . . the same small door the alligator had demolished. When the creature was inside, Mr. Garton put the damaged door over the hole and used a few large bricks to hold it in place.

"That'll keep him until I can get that fixed," Mr. Garton said. "Besides . . . some trucks will arrive tomorrow to begin taking the alligators to zoos. It won't have to hold him for long."

A fast-moving shadow drew my attention, and I turned to see an alligator moving quickly toward one of the cement ponds. The alligator wasn't very big—maybe three feet long—but it sure could move fast. In seconds, it had splashed into the water, and vanished.

"What about the other alligators that have escaped?" I asked. "What are you going to do about them?"

"They'll come back, soon enough," Mr. Garton said. "When I walked over toward the fence, I saw the logs that you had put over the hole. Next to it was another hole under the fence . . . so I think those three alligators dug another hole and came back in. You see, any alligators that get out will realize that it's easier to survive here, in the hatchery, than outdoors in the wild. Here in northern Michigan, the water is much colder than they like. Any alligators that got out—even the littlest ones—are going to make their way back here, where the water in the ponds is warmer and the creatures get fed twice a day. I'll just have to keep my eye out to make sure that more don't escape."

Heather was waiting by the front door of the hatchery, and we started walking toward her.

"Well, we'd better get going," I said. "We've been gone a long time, and we have to check in. Wait until I tell my parents about your alligators!"

Suddenly, another fast-moving shadow appeared.

And another.

Still another.

They were alligators, and, like the one we'd just watched go into the pond, they were about three feet long.

Another one appeared.

Then one came from out of a cement pond.

And another.

They came toward us, circling and snarling, snapping their jaws.

"This is odd," Mr. Garton said. He sounded nervous. "They've never acted this way before."

More appeared. I counted over a dozen alligators all around us.

Soon, we were surrounded, pressed against the outside wall of the hatchery.

"Heather!" Mr. Garton shouted. "Throw some fish into the yard! Quick!"

"I don't have any more!" Heather shouted.

"Go to the freezer and get more!" Mr. Garton ordered. "Hurry!"

Heather vanished as she scurried down the hall to the fish freezer.

I figured she would come back with some fish, throw them toward the alligators, and divert their attention, just like we'd done with Buttons.

Well, that *might* have worked.

But the alligators weren't that patient. Heather had been gone less than ten seconds . . . when the alligators suddenly attacked.

They came at us like a swarm of angry bees, running about on their short, sharp-clawed legs. It happened so fast that I knew there was no way we would be able to get away.

Suddenly, Mr. Garton grabbed me and lifted me up. He placed me on his shoulders . . . just as the ravaging reptiles reached us.

One of them lunged forward, sinking its teeth deep into Mr. Garton's leg. I knew that it must've hurt really bad, but Mr. Garton didn't seem to mind. He didn't scream or wince in pain or anything. He just shook his leg, trying to get the alligator to let go. The alligator relented, letting go and backing off. Another alligator attacked Mr. Garton's other leg, but, again, Mr. Garton didn't cry out in pain or anything. He just started walking, slowly, toward the old fish hatchery building.

"Thick leather boots," he said, as he walked. I was still on his shoulders, out of reach of the swarming alligators. "They go up to my knees, and they sure come in handy. The alligators can't bite through them. Not these alligators, anyway."

Heather appeared at the door with an armload of frozen fish. She had an incredulous look on her face when she saw us.

"Toss the fish over there," Mr. Garton called out, pointing. "Away from us. The alligators will go after the fish and leave us alone."

Heather did as ordered. Just as Mr. Garton said, the alligators quickly picked up the scent of the fish. One by one, they stopped circling around us and headed off in search of fish. Heather kept tossing the fish, and Mr. Garton kept walking.

When we were almost to the door of the hatchery building, he knelt down. I scrambled from his shoulders and onto the ground.

"Man, I'm glad you were wearing those boots," I said. "If you hadn't, those alligators would've torn your legs up!"

"Yes, they would have," Mr. Garton said. "Which is another reason why I'm not going to open up the alligator farm for people to visit. There is too much of a chance of someone getting hurt, and I don't want that."

"Is there a way we can get out of here safely?" Heather asked. I had been wondering the same thing myself.

"Actually, yes," he said. "I have a key to the main gate. That will be safe."

"But our waders are still in the basement of the hatchery," Heather said.

I hadn't thought about that. Actually, I'd forgotten all about my waders.

Mr. Garton stroked his chin. "Okay," he said, "here's what we'll do. I'll go unlock the main gate while you go and get your waders from the main alligator room downstairs. Meet me here by the front door, and I'll have a golf cart waiting. I can drive you to the gate, and you can leave from there."

"But what about other alligators in the wild?" I asked. "What do we do about them?"

"I don't think you'll find any," Mr. Garton replied. "Like I said, they'll come back. Once they've had enough of the cold water, they'll return in a hurry. You don't have anything to worry about."

Do you think I should have worried?

You're right.

I *was* worried, despite what Mr. Garton said.

And soon, I would find out there was good reason for my worry.

34

Heather and I raced tp the basement, found our waders beneath the table, and put them on. I slipped into my vest, and then we trudged back to the front door where Mr. Garton was already waiting for us in a cream-colored golf cart.

"Hop in," he said, and Heather and I scrambled inside and sat. The golf cart whirred to life, and in no time at all we were parked in front of the large, locked gate.

Mr. Garton got out. "Wait here," he said. "I'll unlock the fence, and lock it once you leave." He hopped out of the cart and pulled a wad of keys from his pocket. After a moment, the chain fell away and the gate swung open.

"Okay," he said. "You're on your own."

Heather and I climbed out of the cart and walked to the fence. The boots of our waders scrunched on the hard packed gravel.

"Sorry if we caused any trouble," I said, as we walked through the open gate.

Mr. Garton waved his hand. "You didn't cause any trouble at all. My idea for an alligator farm was silly, anyway. You kids have a good evening."

And with that, Heather and I walked out. Mr. Garton closed and locked the gate behind us. We waved, and he waved back. Then he climbed into the cart and drove off.

"Well, I'm glad that's over with," Heather said.

"Me, too," I said. "We'd better get back. My mom and dad are going to wonder where I've been all day."

"Mine, too," Heather said.

We walked through the brush until we found the small creek. All we had to do was follow it through the forest and the swamp, and it would lead us right back to the AuSable River.

Simple.

After all, Mr. Garton himself had told us that we didn't have anything to worry about.

We followed the creek as it wound through the woods. Heather was careful not to step into the stream, because her waders had a tear and they would leak and fill up with water. I told her that she would have to get wet, anyway, because when she crossed the AuSable River, she would have to wade through. She said no, she wouldn't, and just smiled. I didn't know what she meant by that, and I didn't ask her.

The forest gave way to the swamp, and we were enveloped in shadows. The air became damp, and mosquitos buzzed around our heads. The creek looked like an inky black oil slick with a glossy, frozen surface.

Until I saw something move.

"Heather!" I whispered, grabbing her arm. *"Stop!"*

We stopped walking.

Up ahead, a wake had formed in the creek. It was moving, coming toward us.

I was hoping it was a turtle, or maybe a muskrat. I see a few of those in the AuSable. They are small, rat-like creatures that live near the water. They swim both above and below the surface.

But as the wake drew closer, my nervousness turned into terror.

It was an alligator, all right . . . and this time, there was nowhere for us to go!

Heather saw the alligator's form beneath the surface. She drew in a breath and held it.

We remained motionless, standing next to the creek, as the alligator approached. It was big, too . . . nearly as big as me. If it attacked, we would never get away.

But I didn't think the creature had spotted us yet. If we remained perfectly still—

"Don't move a muscle," I whispered to Heather. I spoke very quietly, barely moving my lips.

The alligator was only a few feet away. Beneath the surface, I could see its full shape, swimming along, being pushed by its powerful tail.

Then, it was right next to us in the water . . . and it went past.

It hadn't spotted us!

We didn't move for nearly a minute, until we were sure that the creature was far up the creek.

Heather heaved a sigh. "That was close," she said.

"Too close," I said.

We made our way through the swamp. Soon we heard the rippling of the AuSable River. Moments later, we were standing on the riverbank.

"Time for you to get wet," I said with a smirk, pointing at the tear in Heather's waders.

Heather shook her head. "I don't think so," she said. "After all . . . I didn't even want to come with you in the first place. It was your idea to go alligator hunting. The way I figure it, you owe me a favor."

"Yeah, right," I said, rolling my eyes. "Like what?"

"Like . . . carrying me across the river."

"You're crazy!" I replied.

"You owe me," she said. "Besides . . . it would be a nice thing for you to do."

"You're probably too heavy," I said.

"I'm waiting," Heather replied impatiently.

"Oh, for crying out loud," I said, giving in.

I spread my arms and picked her up. "Sheesh!" I exclaimed. "You're heavy!"

She scowled and gave me a gentle slap on the arm. "And you better not drop me," she warned.

I started out across the river, carrying Heather in my arms.

"This is much better than getting wet," she said.

"Yeah, well, it's only because—"

I stopped speaking in mid-sentence, and my eyes bulged.

"Oh my gosh!" I shrieked. My jaw fell open. *"There's an alligator, right there!"*

Heather screamed. *"Where?!?! Where?!?!"* she bellowed. *"Where's the alligator?!?!"*

I laughed. "Just kidding," I said.

"You!" she scolded. "I'm going to get you back for that!"

We made it across the river, and I put Heather down.

"Thank you," she said smartly.

"Yeah, don't mention it," I replied.

We followed the trail back to my house, and stopped by the shed.

"I've got to go home," she said. "I can't wait to tell my parents what we did today!"

"Me, too," I said, and I slipped out of my vest and stepped out of my waders.

"See you later," Heather said.

"See ya," I replied.

I quickly stored my gear in the shed and ran to the house.

"Mom!" I yelled, as I walked in the door. "You're not going to believe what we did today!"

Mom was in the kitchen, and I sat down at the counter and explained everything that happened to me. I thought that she wouldn't believe me . . . but she listened to everything I said.

"And that's the truth," I finished. "I even took a couple of pictures with my camera."

"So, you weren't kidding when you said you were going to hunt for alligators," Mom said.

"Nope," I said, shaking my head.

"Well, I'm glad you're not hurt," she replied.

"You . . . you mean you believe me?" I asked.

"Of course," she said. "I'd heard that some guy was going to have an alligator farm at the old fish hatchery. I also heard that it wasn't working out the way he'd planned, so he was going to give his alligators to zoos. I guess that the old fish hatchery is going to be remodeled, and it's going to be a real fish hatchery again."

"That's what Mr. Garton told us," I said. "That's going to be cool!"

"Are you sure that there are no more alligators around?" Mom asked.

"I don't know," I said. "Heather and I saw one in the creek that goes through the swamp. Mr. Garton said that even if a few get out, they always come back. He said that they can't survive very long on their own, because they aren't used to the cold water."

After we ate dinner, I decided to go fly fishing. The evening was warm, and from our living room window, I could see a few trout rising to the surface of the river, feeding on bugs.

I walked to the shed . . . but I stopped before I got there.

On the ground, right in front of the shed, was an alligator . . . and he was as big around as my leg!

I didn't move.

Neither did the alligator.

I took a step back.

The alligator still didn't move.

I took another step back . . . and heard giggling.

Then, I realized what was going on.

"All right, Heather!" I said loudly. "Come out!"

Laughing, holding a hand over her mouth, Heather stepped out from behind the shed.

"I told you I would get you back," she said.

I pointed to the alligator, which was, I now realized, fake. "Where did you get that?" I asked.

"We went into town for dinner," she said, "then we went shopping. I found this rubber alligator at a gift store."

I walked toward it, knelt down, and picked it up. The creature was big, too . . . almost three feet long. "It sure looks real," I said.

"You can have it," Heather said. "I bought it for you."

"Cool!" I exclaimed. "Thanks! I'm going to use it to scare my mom!"

Heather said good-bye, saying that her family was going to get up early in the morning and go to Mackinac Island for a few days. Mackinac Island is a really cool place. It's in Lake Huron, not far from the Mackinac Bridge. In fourth grade, we went there on a class field trip. No cars are allowed on the island, so, to get around, we had to ride in horse carriages or on bicycles! It was a blast.

"See you when you get back," I said. "I hope you have a lot of fun."

"Oh, we will," Heather replied. "See you later."

A few days went by, and I fished a lot. Thankfully, I never saw another alligator . . . except for the rubber alligator that Heather bought for me.

One evening, after dinner, I was fly fishing and I didn't catch a single fish. Sometimes, it's like that. Sometimes, I catch a lot of fish. Other times, I don't catch any at all.

But it was still a lot of fun. And on this particular evening, I met someone who was really interesting.

I waded around a bend, and I saw two people on the shore, fishing from a boat landing that's not far from our house. It was a girl that I hadn't seen before. Her dad was teaching her to fly fish. It was her first time, and she was getting her fly caught in tree branches with almost every cast.

Her dad took his waders out of the car, and I heard him say that he was going to wade downstream and fish for a little while. The girl, who was about my age, told her father she was going to stay at the landing and practice casting.

"Hi," I said, as I wound my fly line onto the reel and approached the landing.

"Hello," she said. "I hope you're better at this than I am." She pointed to the fly rod that she had leaned against her dad's truck.

"Well, it just takes some practice," I said. "I'm Craig Pierce."

"I'm Ashlynn Meyer," she replied. "I'm from Grand Rapids."

"I live here," I said.

"Really?" Ashlynn said. "My family comes up here to vacation. I would love to live up here all the time."

I hiked my thumb over my shoulder. "We live just a little ways upstream. I usually stop fishing at this landing, and walk the trail back home. Usually, I fish late into the night, but I haven't caught any fish, so I'm quitting early."

"Do you ever get scared, walking through the woods after dark?"

"No," I said. Then I remembered the time when Heather had grabbed my leg while hiding in the bushes. "Not usually," I added. "I'm not scared of the woods."

"Me, neither," she said. "But sometimes, I'm afraid of what might be *in* the woods."

I frowned, not knowing what she meant. "What do you mean?" I asked.

"Well, ghouls, for one thing," she replied. "I'm scared of them."

"There is no such thing as ghouls," I said.

Ashlynn nodded. "Yes, there is," she said. "Oh, I know it's hard to believe. Even *I* had a hard time believing it. But they're real . . . sort of."

At first, I thought that Ashlynn was out of her mind.

Ghouls? I thought. *There is no such thing. They are just make-believe.*

But then I remembered the alligators Heather and I had discovered. I suppose if I told people about that, they'd think *I* was crazy.

"What do you mean, 'sort of'?" I asked.

Ashlynn looked away, and then back at me. "Well, they *were* real," she said. "I know they were. But not many other people do."

I was really curious. "Do you mean ghouls, like creepy monsters?"

Ashlynn nodded her head. "Yeah," she said. "They were really scary. My dad's probably going to be fishing for a little while. I'll tell you what happened to me, if you want."

"Yeah," I replied. "It sounds like a freaky story."

"Oh, it's no story," she said. "This really happened to me a few weeks ago."

Still in my waders and vest, I sat down at the edge of the river. Ashlynn sat next to me. She took a breath.

"Okay," she said, "this is really going to sound bizarre, but . . . here goes."

Ashlynn started from the beginning, and once I began to realize that she was telling the truth, I could do nothing but sit in silence and listen to her story.

A story . . . that was real.
A story . . . about *ghouls*.

NEXT IN THE
MICHIGAN CHILLERS SERIES:

#13: GRUESOME GHOULS
OF
GRAND RAPIDS

CONTINUE ON TO READ A FEW
CHILLING CHAPTERS!

I first found out about the wood elves when I was only four or five years old. I was playing in our backyard in Grand Rapids, Michigan, when I saw a very small girl sitting on a branch in a tree.

And when I say 'small', I mean *small*. The girl was only eight or nine inches tall! We started talking, and she told me that she was a wood elf, and that she lived in the forest with many other elves. She looked sort of like a fairy: she was dark-complected, and had thin wings on her back. She uses them to glide through the air. Her hair is dark, like mine, only hers is a lot longer. And the clothing she wears is made from green leaves.

Now, I know this may be hard for *you* to believe, but remember: I was very young. It never occurred to me that wood elves aren't supposed to be real.

When I told my mom and dad about the wood elf, they just laughed. They thought it was cute that I had an 'imaginary' friend. I tried to tell them that the wood elf was real, that I wasn't making it up. Still, Mom and Dad just smiled. My older brother, Rick, just laughed at me.

Well, that was a long time ago. I'm almost twelve now . . . and I've become good friends with a few wood elves. The girl—Lina is her name—comes to my house a couple times a week. She's really smart, and she helps me with my math homework. Two other wood elves, Deepo and Mirak, stop by once in a while, too. There are many more wood elves, they tell me, but they stay in the forest, where it is safer.

And another thing: I'm the only one that can see them, as far as I can tell. Which is probably the reason that mom, dad, and my brother thought that the wood elves were my imaginary friends. They can't see them, and I don't think anyone else can see them, either. I asked Lina about it, and she said that it was because I was special. I didn't know what she meant by that, but I thought that it was cool.

So, I don't talk about the wood elves to anyone, because they would think that I was weird. When Lina comes to my house to visit, I make sure that I speak quietly, so my mom, dad, and brother won't hear. They might think I'm talking to myself. Once, I almost told my best friend, Darius Perry, about the wood elves. But, at the last second, I decided not too. I didn't think he would believe me.

One morning, before I left for school, Lina appeared at my window. I smiled, but my grin quickly faded when I saw the expression on her face. She looked very worried.

I slid open the window, and chilly, April air washed inside. All of the snow had melted the month before, but the mornings were still cold. It would be another few weeks before it got warm and the flowers started to bloom.

"Hi, Lina!" I said.

"Hello, Ashlynn," Lina replied.

"What's wrong?" I asked as she jumped from the window sill to my dresser.

Just then, my bedroom door opened. Lina never moved from the dresser, because she knew that I was the only person who could see her.

"Ten minutes, Ashlynn," Mom said.

"I'll be ready," I replied. I ride the bus to school every day, and my brother and I have to be at our bus stop at eight o'clock, sharp, or we'll miss it.

Mom left, and I turned to Lina.

"Be careful today," she warned.

"Be careful of what?" I asked.

Lina looked around my room, and her wings fluttered a couple of times.

"Just . . . just be on the lookout for anything strange," she said.

"Like what?" I prodded.

Lina really looked nervous. I'd never seen her this way before.

"Creatures," she whispered.

"Creatures?" I echoed. "What kind of creatures?"

"It's a long story," Lina said. "I don't have time to tell you now. But you're able to see us, so you might be able to see the creatures, too."

"What kind of creatures are you talking about, Lina?" I asked.

"Ghouls," Lina said with a shudder and a flutter of her wings.

"Ghouls?" I said, getting a little nervous myself.

"I'll tell you more when you come home from school," Lina replied. "Until then, just be careful. You might be able to see the ghouls. If you can, they'll know it."

This was all very confusing.

"What do they look like?" I asked.

189

Lina shook her head, and her dark hair fell over her shoulders. "Later," she replied. "After you get home from school."

Her wings flitted, and Lina darted to the window sill and peered outside. Then she looked at me.

"Just remember what I told you," she said. "I'll explain everything tonight." Then she leapt from the window, glided through the air, and landed on the branch of the blue spruce that grows near my room. Lina vanished within the thick, needle-covered branches.

I went to school. Throughout the day, I wondered what Lina had meant.

Ghouls? I thought. *What did she mean by that? She's never spoke of ghouls before.*

And I kept my eye out, but I didn't see anything out of the ordinary . . . until I got home.

That's when I discovered something waiting for me, hidden in the shadows of the trees that grew near our garage . . . .

2

That afternoon, the bus dropped me off at the end of our block. Usually, my brother rides the bus with me, but he had basketball practice.

I was alone.

I started to walk home. A cold wind chilled my face, and I shivered beneath my windbreaker. The sky was gray and dreary, and it looked like it might rain at any moment. Trees, their limbs empty of leaves, looked liked bundles of gnarled wires. I couldn't wait for the warm weather to arrive.

I walked along the sidewalk, gazing at the homes that lined the street. We live in a nice neighborhood. Some of the houses are big, and some, like ours, are smaller. Our home is on a dead-end street surrounded by trees. Behind our house, the forest is very thick, and there are many trails that wind through it. In the summer, I go for walks in the woods with my friends. Right now, however, the trails were still muddy from the long, cold winter.

A car went by, and a horn honked. I turned to see Mrs. Walker, our next door neighbor. Mrs. Walker is really nice. She has a big, black dog named Max. Max is very friendly. Once in a while, Mrs. Walker lets me take him for walks. She keeps him in her house, but she has a big fenced-in backyard where the dog runs around and plays. Sometimes, however, he jumps the fence and gets out . . . but he always comes back. I wish we could have a dog, but Dad says no.

I waved to Mrs. Walker, and she waved back. We have a lot of really nice people on our block.

My backpack was getting heavy, and I shifted it to my other shoulder. I had two pages of math homework, and I hoped that Lina would help me with it.

But I was more interested in what she'd promised to tell me about the ghouls. She hadn't told me what they look like, what they do, or anything. She had just warned me to be on the lookout for them.

Oh, well, I thought, as I turned to walk up our driveway. *I'm sure Lina will tell me tonight.*

And that's when I saw it.

A movement. Out of the corner of my eye, I saw something move by the side of our garage where the thick row of cedar shrubs grow. Cedars are like pine trees: they don't lose their leaves or needles in the winter.

And the ones growing next to our garage were tall, too . . . almost as tall as my dad. When my brother and I used to play hide-and-seek, I would hide in the branches all the time.

But what if there was something *else* hiding there right now?

What if it was one of those things that Lina warned me about?

A ghoul?

I stopped walking and stood in the driveway, looking at the cedar shrubs next to the garage.

Nothing moved.

I peered into the thick, spiny foliage, but I couldn't see anything but branches.

And then—

A branch moved!

I didn't know what to do. Should I run inside our house, or should I race into the forest to find Lina?

All too late I realized that I wasn't going to have time to do either. More branches moved and rustled, and a dark shape began to emerge.

Oh my gosh! I thought. *It's what Lina warned me about!*

A ghoul!

3

I opened my mouth and drew in a breath, preparing to let out the loudest scream I could muster. I didn't know what the ghoul was capable of doing, but Lina had seemed very worried about them. I was sure that the creature was probably awful-looking . . . and dangerous.

Then, the ghoul shouted.

"Ouch!" he exclaimed as the branches parted.

I heaved a huge sigh of relief. It wasn't a ghoul! It was Darius Perry!

"What are you doing in there?!?!" I shouted, walking toward him.

Darius looked up and saw me approaching. "My softball," he replied. "I lost it yesterday, when we were playing. I thought it might be in the bushes."

"You scared me," I said. "I . . . I thought you were a—"

I stopped speaking. After all, I couldn't tell Darius that I thought he was a ghoul! He would have thought I was crazy!

"You thought I was a *what?*" Darius asked.

"Oh, nothing," I replied. "You just surprised me, that's all," I said. "Did you find your softball?"

Darius shook his head. "No," he said with a shrug. "I've looked everywhere. I think it's gone for good. Besides," he continued, "I have a ton of math homework. I'd better get started on it."

"I have a lot of math homework, too," I said. "It'll probably take me all night."

"It'll take me longer," Darius said. "You're a lot better at math than I am."

I smiled. I couldn't tell Darius that Lina helped me with my homework. Oh, she didn't give me the answers or anything. That would be cheating. But she showed me how to solve the problems on my own. As a result, I was getting a good grade in math . . . even though I didn't particularly like the subject.

"I'll see you later," Darius said. "If you happen to find my softball, bring it to school tomorrow, will you?"

"Sure," I said. "See you later."

Darius trudged over the lawn and across the street.

I felt silly, being scared like I had been. But, then again, Lina had warned me to be careful, and to be on the lookout for ghouls. I was anxious for her to tell me more about them. I wondered what they looked like.

I walked toward our house . . . but a noise in our garage made me stop.

Turning to look, I didn't see anything out of the ordinary. Mom's red car was parked, and there was an empty space where Dad normally parked his white car. He was still at work.

I peered into the garage for a moment, but I didn't see or hear anything. It was probably just the wind.

But when I turned away, I heard a scratching sound.

Like claws. Claws on cement.

I spun . . . just in time to see a big, dark creature lunging for me!

I dropped my backpack and turned to run . . . when I heard a yelp.

Not just any yelp, either . . . but a happy yelp. A dog's yelp. A yelp that I'd know anywhere.

I turned back around to see Max, Mrs. Walker's dog, bounding toward me. His mouth was open, and his tail was wagging like crazy.

A wave of relief fell over me, and I dropped to my knees as Max approached.

"Hey, buddy!" I said, scratching the dog behind his ears. "You scared me!" I petted his head, and Max instantly rolled onto his back and raised his paws in the air, indicating that he wanted his tummy rubbed.

"You silly thing," I said, scratching his belly. Max closed his eyes, enjoying the attention. "Come on. Let's get you home."

I stood, and Max followed. Then I picked up my backpack and carried it to the porch.

"Mom!" I hollered, after I'd opened the door. "I'm going to take Max over to Mrs. Walker's house."

"How was school today?" Mom asked from the kitchen.

"Fine," I replied. "Same as yesterday."

"Come right home after you take Max home," she said.

"I will," I said. "I'll be right back."

I dropped my backpack on the floor and closed the door.

"Come on, Max," I said. "Let's get you home."

I began walking across the yard, and Max followed. I wondered how the dog had escaped. Usually, he jumped the fence. But, once in a while, he would dig a hole under it. That made Mrs. Walker mad, because it ruined the lawn.

I stopped at the curb to make sure there were no cars coming. Then I continued across the street. Max sniffed at the pavement like a bloodhound.

When we reached the sidewalk on the other side of the street, Max suddenly stopped. His ears stood straight up, and he had a puzzled look on his face.

"What's up, you silly dog?" I asked.

Max gave me a quick glance and wagged his tail, then continued looking around curiously.

I looked around the neighborhood. At the end of the block, a car was backing out of a driveway. Other than that, there wasn't much going on.

"Come on," I said, and started walking. I could see Mrs. Walker's house, and her car in the driveway.

Max followed. Whatever he'd heard or spotted, he must have forgot about it.

In no time at all, we arrived at Mrs. Walker's house. I skirted the side of her garage, intending to let Max into the backyard through the gate. Then,

I would go to the front door and tell Mrs. Walker that I'd returned her dog.

But when I reached the fence and looked into the yard, I stopped and stared. What I saw was awful . . . and I knew, right then, that something was very, very wrong . . . .

5

In Mrs. Walker's backyard, a large hole had been ripped through the chain link fence. I knew right away that Max couldn't have done it, because the fence was made of metal. There was no way Max—or any dog, for that matter—could have done it. The fence was shredded, like it had been ripped apart by some sort of—

Monster.

That's what I thought, anyway. The fence had been peeled back and torn apart, exposing frayed, jagged points. Something very strong had created a large hole in the fence.

Max was standing obediently by my side, waiting for me to open the gate.

"No," I said to the dog. "Let's go around front. I can't put you in the backyard, because you'll just get out again."

I walked, followed by Max, to the front of the house, where I rang the doorbell. Mrs. Walker came to the door a moment later.

"Well, if it isn't Ashlynn Meyer," she said with a smile. But when she saw Max on the porch, her smile faded. "Max," she scolded gently, pointing to the dog and wagging her finger. "Did you get out of the backyard again?"

"What happened to your fence, Mrs. Walker?" I asked.

Mrs. Walker looked puzzled. "What's wrong with it?" she asked. It was clear that she was unaware that her fence was damaged.

"There's a big hole ripped in it," I replied. "I think that's how Max got out this time. Go look. I'll meet you back there."

Mrs. Walker opened the door, and Max bounded inside. I turned and leapt off the porch, sprinting over the lawn and driveway, rounding the side of the garage and to the backyard. I stopped at the gate, lifted the latch, and pulled it open. Then I closed it behind me and walked to where the fence had been damaged.

Mrs. Walker was already there. Her hands were on her hips, and she looked shocked.

"How in the world did this happen?" she asked. "Max couldn't possibly have done it. The fence looks like it's been torn apart by a bear."

Which was unlikely. We have bears in Michigan, but not in the city of Grand Rapids. And I couldn't think of any other animal big or strong enough to rip apart a metal fence.

"Well, I suppose I'd better call the police to report the damage," Mrs. Walker said. "Until it gets fixed, I'm going to have to keep an eye on Max, so he doesn't run off again. Thank you for bringing him back."

"No problem," I replied with a shrug. "I'd better get home, though."

I said good-bye to Mrs. Walker and let myself out through the gate. Before I walked away, I turned around and took one last look at the torn fence.

Lina's soft voice echoed in my head.

Ghouls, she had said. *You might be able to see the ghouls. If you can, they'll know it.*

I have to admit, I was a little scared.

Did a ghoul rip a hole in the fence? I wondered. *What do they look like? How big are they? Are they vicious?*

I turned to head home . . . and received the answer to all of my questions.

Standing in the driveway, looking right at me, was the most horrible, hideous beast I had ever seen in my life.

He was huge . . . and when he realized that I had spotted him, he attacked!

About the author

Johnathan Rand is the author of the best-selling **'Chillers'** series, now with over 2,000,000 copies in print. In addition to the **'Chillers'** series, Rand is also the author of the **'Adventure Club'** series, including **'Ghost in the Graveyard'**, **'Ghost in the Grand'**, and **'The Haunted Schoolhouse'**, three collections of thrilling, original short stories. When Mr. Rand and his wife are not traveling to schools and book signings, they live in a small town in northern lower Michigan with their two dogs, Abby and Lily Munster. He is currently working on more 'Chillers', as well as a new series for younger readers entitled **'Freddie Fernortner, Fearless First Grader'**. His popular website features hundreds of photographs, stories, and art work. Visit:

www.americanchillers.com

All AudioCraft books are proudly printed, bound, and manufactured in the United States of America, utilizing American resources, labor, and materials.

USA